W9-CDJ-865

ENCORE!

ENCORE!

The inside story
of the Atlanta Braves'
second consecutive
National League championship

BY I.J. ROSENBERG
AND THE PHOTOGRAPHY STAFF
OF THE ATLANTA JOURNAL-CONSTITUTION

Editors: Robert Mashburn, Al Tays
Cover design: Jill Dible
Photo editor: Rich Addicks
Photo printing: M. Chris Hunt, Pam Prouty
Cover photos: Reneé Hannans (front), Frank Niemeir (back)
Sports editor: Glenn Hannigan
Production: David Powell, Bill Willoughby, Olin Gordon, Chuck Turlington, Joann LeMastus
and the Composing-Camera Color Staff

Published and distributed by Longstreet Press
2140 Newmarket Parkway
Suite 118
Marietta, Georgia 30067

Copyright © 1992 The Atlanta Journal and The Atlanta Constitution

All rights reserved. No part of this book may be reproduced
in any form or by any means without the prior written permission of the publisher,
excepting brief quotations used in connection with reviews,
written specifically for inclusion in a magazine or newspaper.

This book was produced on Macintosh IIfx computers
using Quark XPress software and a Scitex color system.

First edition

Manufactured in the United States of America
ISBN: 1-56352-062-1

CONTENTS

ACKNOWLEDGMENTS

Another season. Another book.

I'm grateful to many people, but none more than editor Al Tays and book designer Robert Mashburn. As they did for last year's "Miracle Season," they logged countless hours to help complete this project in time for the holidays, sacrificing time with their families for almost a month. So special thanks go to their wives, Vicki and Claudia.

The photo staff of *The Atlanta Journal-Constitution,* as always, shot many breathtaking photos, and photo editor Rich Addicks combed through thousands of frames of film to choose the pictures you see in this book. Chris Hunt and Pam Prouty printed more than 200 photos.

I want to offer a special heartfelt thanks to Longstreet Press publisher Chuck Perry, who guided the project from start to finish.

I also received a lot of support from *Journal-Constitution* publisher Jay Smith, who pushed hard for this book and was always there when I needed him. The same can be said for editor Ron Martin and managing editor John Walter, who have been responsible for the expanded coverage of this team.

A special acknowledgment goes to my department head, Glenn Hannigan, and to *Journal* sports editor Furman Bisher, whose advice and encouragement I will never tire of seeking.

There is also a host of family, friends and co-workers who have been extremely helpful: Bunny and Charles Rosenberg; Marvin and Miriam Botnick; Sammy and Nora (soon-to-be) Rosenberg; Karen, Atsmon and Jonathan Paz; Harris and Geri Botnick; Mike Tierney; Mike Fish; Bobby Clay; Scott Peacocke; Mike Luck; Terence Moore; Rick Zabell; Jim Smith; Gerry Overton; Mark Bradley; Al Smith; Joe Strauss; Len Pasquarelli; Vince Verdi; Glenn Sheeley; J.C. Clemons; Steve Hummer; Jonell McFadden; Tom Cornelison; Sylvia King; Ken Blankenship; Tom Whitfield; and Bill Whitley. And I can't forget my two Nanas and grandfather.

And of course, thanks to Francisco Cabrera, whose game-winning hit in the ninth inning of Game 7 of the playoffs made this book a reality.

I. J. ROSENBERG

To Beth Ann, Lindsey and Ashley, the MVPs on my team

ANOTHER MIRACLE

THE FEELING THAT RUSHED THROUGH ME IN THE FINAL minutes of Wednesday, Oct. 14, 1992, was much like the one I had some 18 years ago. On that April night in 1974, I sat with my grandparents near the third-base line in Atlanta-Fulton County Stadium and watched the great Hank Aaron hit his 715th home run to break Babe Ruth's record.

Now, I was sitting in the press box, watching some 50,000 people break into utter pandemonium. A seldom-used catcher named Francisco Cabrera, who had spent most of the 1992 baseball season in the minor leagues, had just delivered one of the biggest hits in the history of baseball to give the Atlanta Braves their second straight National League pennant. Cabrera's two-out, two-run single in the bottom of the ninth inning of the seventh and final game of the NL Championship Series rescued the Braves from a 2-1 deficit against the Pittsburgh Pirates and sent them into the World Series against the Toronto Blue Jays.

When slow-footed Sid Bream slid across home plate with the winning run just a few minutes before midnight, I had about 30 minutes to pound out a game story for the Atlanta Journal-Constitution that captured this incredible scene: Bream lying on his back near the plate, buried under an avalanche of joyous teammates.

An unlikely hero, Francisco Cabrera, hoisted the NL Championship trophy in a jubilant locker room following the Braves' dramatic Game 7 victory.

Photo: RICH MAHAN

Sid Bream rumbled around third and slid across home plate with the winning run, barely beating the tag by Pirates catcher Mike LaValliere.

FRANK NIEMEIR

But for about a minute, I had to catch my breath. For two years I had managed not to let the Braves affect me emotionally. But long before I became a sportswriter, I was a Braves fan. I grew up in Atlanta, watching the likes of Aaron, Phil Niekro and Dale Murphy.

Besides, you couldn't watch this scene and not be affected. Because of the circumstances that Cabrera's hit overcame — the Braves were one out from blowing a three-games-to-one lead to the Pirates — this was arguably the most memorable sports night the city has ever seen.

As it turned out, it was the highlight of the season. The Braves won the World Series opener three nights later, then lost the next three games. A win in Game 5 in Toronto brought the Series back to Atlanta, but the Braves had exhausted their supply of miracles. They produced their last one in Game 6 when they tied the Jays in the bottom of the ninth, but finally lost in the 11th.

In contrast to 1991, when the Braves lost the Series to the Minnesota Twins on a 1-0 defeat in Game 7, this time coming up short hurt a lot more. The previous year's Braves, who rose from worst in the NL West in 1990 to first in '91, weren't expected to be in the Series, much less win it. But the '92 team faced high expectations. Now they had to live with being the first team to lose consecutive World Series since the Dodgers did it in 1977-78. But if they showed me and millions of others anything this season, it was their ability to bounce back. I wouldn't count them out next year.

One thing that should be different in '93 is their play early in the season. The '92 Braves started slowly, which wasn't a surprise considering all the autograph shows and personal appearances they made in the off-season. This time, they've vowed, will be different.

Back in February, at the beginning of spring training, I decided to keep a diary. Over the course of the season it would become filled with the kind of day-to-day goings on that are typical of a major-league ballclub, but that rarely make their way into the newspaper. It didn't take a lot of foresight to realize that such a journal would come in handy should this club make it back to the World Series. If another book would be written to follow up last year's "Miracle Season," I wanted it to be a more in-depth look at the daily life of a professional sports team.

"Encore!" is that book. I hope you enjoy reading it as much as I have enjoyed writing it.

MARLENE KARAS

Around the city, fans could hardly believe their eyes as they watched Francisco Cabrera drive home Sid Bream with the winning run.

CHAPTER 1

THE SPRING OF PROBLEMS

FRIDAY, FEB. 21

IT ISN'T QUITE 8 A.M. IN WEST PALM BEACH, FLA., AS THE white rental Chrysler LeBaron turns onto Hank Aaron Way. Technically, it's still winter, but that's a relative term in this part of the world, where anything under 70 degrees sends panicked locals scurrying to the malls in search of parkas and mittens. The calendar says the vernal equinox and the first day of spring are still a month off, but my itinerary for today begs to differ. Besides, here in South Florida, the official harbinger of spring is the first sighting of an out-of-town sportswriter.

The Municipal Stadium parking lot is practically deserted. Only a few members of the Atlanta Braves have arrived. Over on the six fields of this spring training complex, which the Braves share with the Montreal Expos, the sprinklers are on.

The parking setup here is an example of the contradictions of baseball's class structure. The best spaces — those right next to the team offices — go to the front office types, general manager John Schuerholz, president Stan Kasten, manager Bobby Cox, etc. The players have to park on the far side of the stadium. But who do you think makes more — the top-paid executive or the

Tom Glavine, coming off a Cy Young season, was popular among autograph seekers in West Palm Beach.

Photo: WALTER STRICKLIN

top-paid player? The salaries of people like Kasten and Schuerholz and Cox are pretty much matters of speculation, because club executives don't have a union publicizing what they make the way players do. But you can bet the mortgage that a Terry Pendleton, the 1991 NL Most Valuable Player, or a Tom Glavine, the '91 NL Cy Young Award winner as the league's top pitcher, both of whom make about $3 million a year, can afford to pick up a lot more dinner tabs than a Kasten or a Schuerholz or a Cox.

The cars in both lots provide another clue. The execs are driving brand new Toyota Camrys, this spring's rental car of choice. A Camry isn't exactly a piece of trash, but it isn't exactly Ron Gant's Lamborghini, either.

One space in front of the offices isn't likely to get a lot of use this spring. It's reserved for Ted Turner, the cable-TV magnate who owns the Braves. Ted doesn't get down to West Palm much anymore, maybe once or twice a spring, but nobody wants to be the guy who was parked in that space on The Day Ted Showed Up. Ted's a lot calmer than he used to be, and he might think it was a gutsy move. Then again, he might not.

For about a half-second, there's a temptation to pull into the space myself. There's no way Ted's going to be here this early. The Braves would view it as a pretty good joke, something to break the ice on the first day back on the job. Then again, they might not. Oh well, there are plenty of other spaces.

A closer spot would have been nice only because it would have meant a shorter distance to lug these two over-the-shoulder bags. Baseball writer? Try pack mule. I've got a laptop computer, Tandy 1500 HD, with power pack and heavy-duty cord, a voice-activated microcassette tape recorder with extra batteries, a dozen Reporter's Notebook steno pads, a cellular phone and a host of books containing baseball statistics and records. There's the "Complete Baseball Record Book," the National League "Green Book" (the yearly guide to all the NL teams), the companion American League "Red Book," a 1992 "Baseball Guide" and "Baseball Register," the latter of which contains complete lifetime statistics on every player currently in the major leagues. I'll pick up a new Braves media guide when I get inside and won't let it out of my sight thereafter. Where I draw the line is the "Baseball Encyclopedia," which is about the size of a small microwave, only heavier. It's good for stats on retired players (it lists everyone who ever played in the majors), but my use for it would be limited at best, and they've got one back at the office in Atlanta.

Public relations director Jim Schultz is already here, already on the phone. The only time it isn't ringing is when Schultz is talking on it. Everybody wants a piece of the Braves after their miracle season of 1991, in which they went from last place in their division the year before to winning it — worst to first. Schultz's regular staff from Atlanta won't be here for a while, so he has hired a temporary aide, an older gent named Buck Kinard, who used to be a local sportscaster.

WALTER STRICKLIN

More than any other time, players are accessible for autographs during the spring.

Kinard likes to talk.

This is the first of 217 days I will spend with the Braves this season, my second year covering the club as the beat writer for the Atlanta Journal-Constitution. It will be tough to top last year, when the Braves' season didn't end until the 10th inning of the seventh game of the World Series. Unfortunately for them and their fans, it ended with them on the losing end of a 1-0 score. Sports Illustrated called it the greatest World Series ever. That wasn't much consolation for the Braves, who are eager to get back into it this year — only with a different ending.

My job description is simple. Be here at all hours, break news stories and write everything that may appeal to the paper's readers. Show up early, leave late. I'm typically the last one to leave each day.

The first order of business is to see who's in the clubhouse already. Pitchers and catchers are due to report today, but they don't have to show up at the park, just phone and say they're in town. Most of them will make an appearance anyway.

There's a surprise waiting around the corner of the clubhouse — about 50 people, looking for autographs.

"Hey, could you tell Deion to come out?" says one, referring to Deion Sanders, who plays outfield for the Braves and cornerback for the Atlanta Falcons. Since Bo Jackson got hurt, Sanders is the No. 1 two-sport athlete in America, and America seems to be crazy for two-sport athletes. It also doesn't hurt Sanders that he's got a ton of talent, especially as a football player, where he might be the best cornerback in the NFL, or that he's flashy. These people love him.

Only one problem. Deion's still back in Atlanta.

Spring training clubhouses tend to be Spartan affairs, small cinder-block squares. This one isn't much bigger than your average suburban basement, and it has to accommodate 60 or so players.

Today it's empty except for assistant equipment manager Casey Stevenson and two of his "clubbies," baseball's version of gofers. They wash jerseys, clean spikes, and cater to whatever whim a player may have. Stevenson, a quiet, large man, runs the show. Technically, he answers to traveling secretary Bill Acree, but Stevenson typically gives the orders. The players give him a lot of respect. His diligence pays off, too, for at the end of the season, he would get a check from every player, sometimes as much as $2,000.

No surprise that Cox is in. He often gets to the park just after sunrise. His office is a small cinder-block room with a toilet and shower and a closet with no door. Cox is dressed in long, thin white socks, called "sanitary socks," a gray jersey with long blue sleeves (a garment generically referred to as "baseball sleeves" because it's worn under a short-sleeved baseball uniform in cold weather) and underwear that stretches down almost to his knees. It's baseball's version of skivvies. All he needs to go out in public are the uniform pants and shirt, but it's hot in here.

Cox can be very personable, but he's about as quotable as a gerani-

JOEY IVANSCO

One advantage of spring training — refreshments are cheaper than at Atlanta–Fulton County Stadium, but not by much.

um. At one point later in the season, my boss will issue an edict —
only half-kiddingly — that henceforth no Bobby Cox quotes are to
appear in the paper. Actually, that probably would suit Cox fine. He's
deliberately dull. He hates being a focus of attention. If the paper
never mentioned his name again, he'd be ecstatic. Well, happy. I'm
not sure Bobby Cox ever gets ecstatic.

On this morning, however, Cox is merely shooting the bull. He's
talking about something other than baseball — the subject is a farm-
house and man-made lake he's building in North Georgia — so he's
relaxed, smiling. Nobody's asked him about Charlie Leibrandt and
Kirby Puckett in a couple of months.

There's no need, because Leibrandt is here. He's the veteran pitch-

WALTER STRICKLIN

Pitchers and catchers loosened up in the Braves' indoor facility before taking the field for the first time.

er who, coming into Game 6 of last year's World Series in an unfamiliar relief role, gave up a game-winning home run to the Twins' Puckett. After that game, in which the Twins tied the Series 3-3 before winning it the next night, a disconsolate Leibrandt sat slumped in front of his locker, his hands covering his tear-stained face. No one wanted to ask him about the pitch, but that's part of a sportswriter's job. So we did. But he hadn't talked that night, nor had he talked to any writers about it in the offseason. This is the perfect time. He has had all winter to compose himself, to learn how to deal with it.

"I wonder what *you* want to talk about," he says, spotting me. "All right, it's time to talk about it."

My first thought is that this is going to make a heck of a story. Any time you can get a person to open up about an emotional subject, it makes for compelling reading. But what Leibrandt tells me is beyond compelling. Shortly after the end of Game 7 last October, his wife's father died. Suddenly, Kirby Puckett's home run doesn't seem like such a sensitive issue anymore.

"Honestly, I was more worried about how my wife was doing than one lousy mistake in a baseball game," Leibrandt says. "That made my heartache go away. I don't like to relive it. I still don't feel comfortable talking about this.

"I didn't come through in a clutch time. But there are a lot of us on this team that feel that way, a lot of guys who in a lot of situations had a chance to finish the Series off not only in Game 6 but also in Game 7. I'm not going to bear the brunt of us losing."

I won't ask Leibrandt about Puckett again.

SUNDAY, FEB. 23

The last two days have been easy. Pitchers and catchers hit the field early, throw a little, run a little and then head for the golf course or fishing pond. In the morning, while I'm working on a piece on catcher Greg Olson, Schultz comes into the office and says he needs someone to fill in for Mike Stanton at a local golf tournament. Stanton, a relief pitcher, has a sore arm. The Olson story doesn't have to be done until 9 tonight, and my clubs are in my trunk (always be prepared, that's my motto), so sure, I'll play. Besides, Olson's going to be there, too.

The tournament is being played at Breakers West, one of seemingly thousands of top-flight golf courses in Palm Beach County. When I arrive, I'm greeted by an older man who grabs my hand and says, "Hello, Mike." He doesn't seem pleased when I tell him I'm just a fill-in. But Harold Alfond, who turns out to be the owner of Dexter Shoes and a 20 percent share of the Boston Red Sox, warms up to me after I make putts for birdies on the first two holes.

As a bonus, I get a good Olson anecdote out of the outing. On one hole, everyone is forced to hit his tee shot blindfolded. Olson knocks his 250 yards straight down the middle.

MONDAY, FEB. 24

Baseball may be their profession, but golf is the passion for a lot of these guys. Today the top three starting pitchers, John Smoltz, Steve Avery and Tom Glavine, have talked Cox into letting them leave practice early so they can go play golf with three pros — Lee Trevino from the Senior PGA Tour, and Mark Calcavecchia and Ken Green from the PGA Tour. Green, who lives near here, has set it up, and about 500 people will come out to the course to watch.

During the morning workout, Smoltz is so excited he can't concentrate. Several times he asks reporters what time it is. Smoltz is the best golfer on the team, with the possible exception of Leibrandt, and he's eager to match his game against the guys who do it for a living.

"When Smoltz stops pitching, he can take up this game for a living."

STEVE AVERY, AFTER WATCHING JOHN SMOLTZ SHOOT 70 IN A ROUND OF GOLF WITH THREE TOURING PROS

WALTER STRICKLIN

12

ENCORE!

THE 1992 ATLANTA BRAVES

He says his handicap is a seven, which means he should shoot a 79 on a par-72 course. Instead, he shoots a 2-under-par 70, including a 60-foot chip-in on the ninth hole. "I'll tell you what," says Avery, who shoots an 84, "when John stops pitching he can think about taking up this game for a living." Says Smoltz, "I have never, ever shot like that." The three pros beat Smoltz, but not by much. Trevino, one of the best players of all time and now the top dog on the Senior Tour for pros 50 and older, shoots a 66, as did Calcavecchia. Green is next with a 67. Glavine brings up the rear with an 89 and isn't happy about it. He hates to lose at anything.

WEDNESDAY, FEB. 26

The first day of the full squad practice is upon us. The position players have been coming in over the last few days. First baseman Brian Hunter arrives after spending a couple of days in a suburban Atlanta jail cell, a result of his second drunken-driving arrest.

The Braves are worried about Hunter. They've sent him to an alcohol rehabilitation program, but its effect is doubtful. Hunter won't commit himself to giving up drinking. "If I happen to drink, I won't drive," he says. But he seems genuinely affected by his jail time. "It woke me up," he says. "I'm going to calm myself off the field. Sleeping was the worst part. I just wanted to find out if I was an alcoholic."

THURSDAY, FEB. 27

The first big news of camp: Gant has been switched from center field to left and Otis Nixon from left to center. Left field is often the position where a manager plays his weakest defensive outfielder, since there's less ground to cover than in center and fewer long throws than in right. (There's no comparable throw to the one the right fielder must make to third base.) Gant isn't considered weak defensively, and he's plenty fast — just not as fast as Nixon. Gant, who has been shuttled around to several positions during his career — he came up to the Braves as a second baseman — says he has no objections to the move. "I realize Otis Nixon is a more natural center fielder," he says.

Gant, however, has not yet been informed of the move by Cox. When I brought it up, it was news to him. Even though he knows I know, Cox won't say anything until he's talked to Gant. This is a typical game played by baseball management types, including Cox and Schuerholz. Last year, when the two agreed on a contract extension for Cox, the Journal-Constitution knew it even before Cox's wife did. Once Schuerholz found that out, he made an early announcement, rather than let the newspaper have an exclusive. On another occasion, I had written a story about Sanders possibly leaving the Falcons to return to the Braves part time. Schuerholz was so angry, he didn't talk to me the next day. He never said the story was wrong, just that "I was upset because of all the phone calls that I got when your story ended up on the front page."

The first big news of camp: Ron Gant has been switched from center field to left and Otis Nixon from left to center.

14

WALTER STRICKLIN

MONDAY, MARCH 2

Finally some news with a bite. Right fielder David Justice has refused to pose for the team picture. He's upset over the club's contract offer. Schuerholz is furious, saying, "If he was *my* son, he wouldn't act this way."

Schuerholz won't leave it at that, either. "If he doesn't want to act like a member of the team, if he doesn't want to be shoulder to shoulder with his teammates, that is entirely his choice. His teammates are asked to do these things, and they do. His teammates sense that he's setting himself apart from the rest of the team. David is not special. Every player in the history of this game has participated in things that the club has asked them to do. Shoot, George Brett is a Hall of Famer and he did it all, and never were there any questions being asked."

Justice, a talented but moody player beginning his third year in the majors, is a controversial figure on this team. The Braves are basically divided into three camps on the Justice question. A few players protect him, primarily Hunter and Gant. Another group, consisting primarily of veterans, ignores him. And a third group doesn't like him, but will say so only behind his back. More than a few Braves fit into this category.

Justice also has had some run-ins with the media. Last season he carried around an electronic notebook, in which he kept the names of reporters and what they wrote about him. If he felt a story was negative, he'd cut that reporter off. I was probably No. 1 on his hit list,

As some Braves clowned around on photo day, teammate David Justice was AWOL.

our differences stemming from the incident that earned Hunter his first DUI arrest. Late in the 1991 season, Justice had been out for a time with Hunter and another young outfielder, Keith Mitchell, and the latter two got into separate auto accidents that night, both resulting in DUIs, while they were driving home. Justice had been very candid in talking about the evening the next day, but he was upset about the headline on the story: *"Night on town with Justice turns sour for Hunter and Mitchell."* I admitted the headline could be taken to imply that Justice had a larger role in his teammates' misadventures than he really did (he was home in bed by the time Hunter and Mitchell were being arrested). But a bigger problem was Justice's conviction that I had written the headline myself, with malicious intent. Writers don't write headlines. Editors do. But Justice would not be swayed.

He was convinced I was out to get him. One night in Cincinnati, after he hit a game-winning homer, he refused to talk to a group of reporters until I had left.

Whatever his personality, Justice was one of the Braves' stars, and they wanted him to patch up his image. They hired a "media consultant," Andrea Kirby, who had worked with several National League clubs, including Montreal, New York and St. Louis. She held seminars for players to teach them how to deal with — some would say manipulate — the media. The advice was particularly good for young players, who were often shy. But Kirby admitted Justice was one of her main projects. Guess who didn't attend the first seminar?

In a last resort, Schuerholz went to Pendleton, the unofficial team captain and elder statesman, and asked him to talk to Justice. The meeting never came about.

WEDNESDAY, MARCH 4

Time for the season's first drug talk, given by team doctor David Watson. According to a couple of witnesses, the meeting lasted an hour, and a few players were starting to doze off. Two players who paid attention were Nixon and Lonnie Smith, both of whom have spent time in rehab centers. Nixon missed the 1991 stretch drive, the playoffs and the World Series after testing positive for cocaine, and still has to sit out the first 18 days of this season. Smith never has been suspended, but he entered drug rehab when he was in St. Louis in 1984. Smith is hard to figure. A reporter never knows when he's going to get Cooperative Lonnie, Silent Lonnie or Angry Lonnie. On the subject of drug rehab, which is something a lot of players don't want to talk about, he's very candid. "After I stopped going [to rehab]," he says, "I wanted to get as close as possible with my family. I talk about it often with them. It reminds me that if I ever went back [to doing drugs], I'd be dead."

After workouts, however, he took out a big squirt gun and started shooting at reporters, trying to soak people's crotches. It's the typical kind of junior high type humor that goes on in the clubhouse, but

"After I stopped going [to rehab], I wanted to get as close as possible with my family. I talk about it often with them. It reminds me that if I ever went back, I'd be dead."

LONNIE SMITH,
AFTER A LECTURE
TO THE TEAM
ABOUT DRUGS

WALTER STRICKLIN

Rumors that GM John Schuerholz wanted to trade Jeff Treadway came to a quick halt when Treadway had to undergo surgery on his right hand.

there's an edge to it. I wouldn't describe it as friendly kidding. Over the next few days I would be on the lookout for that squirt gun. Once, I would even go into Smith's locker and hide it, but a clubbie quickly found it and put it back. The clubbies are afraid of Smith.

The Jeff Treadway rumors already have begun. Schuerholz has decided to trade the backup second baseman before the season starts. Treadway had been the starter at second, but lost his job when Mark Lemke turned into Joe DiMaggio in the 1991 World Series. Management figures Lemke, a career .225 hitter who hit .417 in the Series against the Twins, now has the confidence to carry his offensive improvement over to the regular season, and he's already regarded as Treadway's superior defensively. The problem with dealing Treadway, however, is that you don't want to just give him away. He hit .320 in 106 games in '91, and his career average — .285 — is 60 points higher than Lemke's.

Treadway knows his days as a Brave are numbered, especially since

Cox is a big Lemke man, but he's careful about what he says to reporters. If he goes, he'll be missed, because he's one of the most pleasant players in the clubhouse.

"I'm a little surprised they're so ready to do it," Treadway says. "I've worked hard to improve myself. Mark had a good second half and a good postseason. He seized the opportunity. I know Lemke is viewed as being better defensively, but I don't subscribe to that fact. I hope [a trade] will be soon."

Word is out that the Baltimore Orioles are interested in Treadway. But before a deal can be consummated, he undergoes surgery to fuse two joints in his right hand, and all possible trades are off.

While Treadway is worried about a trade, others are concerned about their contracts. Specifically, those with less than three years of major league experience.

The way the contract rules are set up in major league baseball under the Basic Agreement between labor (the players) and management (the owners), players have virtually no bargaining leverage for their first three seasons in the majors. Clubs have to pay them the major league minimum salary, $109,000, but that's it. After three years (somewhat more quickly for some players, according to a complicated statistical arrangement), players are eligible to file for salary arbitration. To most of the game's executives, that is the most profane two-word phrase in the English language, and the source of all of baseball's financial woes.

Salary arbitration is a process by which, when a player and his team cannot come to an agreement on a salary, they each submit a proposed salary to an independent arbitrator. The arbitrator listens to arguments from both sides, then picks one figure or the other. Generally speaking, players love arbitration, owners hate it. Why? Because the decisions are made based on comparisons to other players with similar time of service, so when one player gets a high salary, it tends to raise those of other players who have been in the majors about the same amount of time. It's as if the scale can go up, but never down.

Avery is one of the unhappy ones. He has only one year and 113 days of major-league service (172 days constitutes a full year), so he has no leverage. After the monster season he had in 1991 — 18-8, plus two 1-0 victories over the Pirates in the playoffs — you'd think he'd be in line to become one of the team's top-paid players. But unlike pro football, which pays top money to first-round draft choices and franchise quarterbacks, baseball makes its youngsters wait for their money. Of course, once baseball players get enough experience, the best ones get paid far more than the best football players.

Avery understands the situation, but he doesn't like it. "What am I going to do?" he repeats a reporter's question. "I don't know. I think what is going to hurt the club is when they negotiate in the future. If they think I'm going to forget about this, they're crazy."

Justice, who came only 13 runs batted in short of 100 last season despite missing 53 games, has two full years in the majors, so he's not

"Walk out? I'm not going anywhere. I'll be here the whole time."

DAVID JUSTICE, WHEN ASKED HOW HE WOULD RESPOND TO THE BRAVES' SALARY STRUCTURE

JOEY IVANSCO

looking at any huge raise, either. "I leave it to my agent," he says. "Walk out? I'm not going anywhere. I'll be here the whole time. It's hard for me to say what's fair. I'm asked to hit 30 home runs and drive in 100 runs, and I'm the lowest-paid fourth-place hitter in the league. I feel I should get something for the amount of responsibility they put on me."

The task of negotiating with all these unhappy campers falls to Schuerholz's assistant, Dean Taylor. He and Schuerholz say they've got a scale that maxes out at $500,000. But the euphoria of 1991 seems to have gotten to them, for sure enough, Justice ends up getting $555,000, a raise of $258,500 from $296,500. Guess that team photo thing has been forgotten. More likely, it was a meeting between Schuerholz and Justice and his agent, Eric Goldschmidt. Schuerholz can't stand Goldschmidt, but winning popularity contests isn't an

A spring portrait of award winners: Terry Pendleton (MVP), Steve Avery (NLCS MVP), Tom Glavine (Cy Young) and Bobby Cox (Manager of the Year).

agent's job.

In the end, Schuerholz and Taylor would end up shelling out near-ly $35 million in salaries for the 1992 Braves, a 78 percent increase over the approximately $20 million they paid to essentially the same roster in '91.

Look at the top five guys in terms of percentage of raise:

1. Nixon, a 350 percent raise, from $585,000 to $2.635 million. He was a free agent, and the Braves had to outbid the California Angels for him.

2. Smoltz, a 330 percent raise from $355,000 to $1.525 million. It was his first time eligible for arbitration.

3. Glavine, a 305 percent raise from $722,000 to $2.925 million.

WALTER STRICKLIN

*Pitching coach
Leo Mazzone,
in charge of one of the
best starting rotations
in baseball, met with
his pupils daily.*

His second time eligible for arbitration, plus he was coming off a Cy Young season.

4. Blauser, a 230 percent raise from $280,000 to $925,000. First time eligible for arbitration.

5. Avery, a 228 percent raise from $110,000 to $355,000. Not yet eligible for arbitration, but coming off a great season. So Avery gets the biggest percentage increase of any of the no-leverage players.

Enough about money. Nixon and Sanders went fishing today. Most of the players like to spend their off-time playing golf, but these two outfielders, who are competing for the starting center field job, spend virtually all their spare moments at a lake near their condominium. Sometimes they let Olson tag along.

As with everything these ballplayers do, they bring a spirit of intense competition to fishing. And they love to rag each other. Sanders: "I don't even know how they [Nixon's fish] fit on his hook, they were so small." Nixon: "He talks like Muhammad Ali."

Sanders says fishing relaxes him, lets him forget about contract negotiations or trying to play two pro sports. He likes to say he'll be the first black man to have a TV fishing show. He's already got a couple of titles picked out: "Tight Lining and Prime Timing" or "Fishin' in the 'Hood."

He also gets a kick out of two of his teammates' fishing foibles. "I get to laugh at Avery when he gets his line hung up in the tree," he says. "I like to watch Olson, who has the best rod, best bait and best lures and fishing knowledge, not catch any fish."

Olson, one of the nicest guys of all time, won't — pardon the pun — take the bait. "It was great," he says, "when I took that cane pole away from Deion and gave him his first Zebco reel and fiberglass pole." That's typical Olson: a sincere expression of happiness for someone else, plus a subtle plug for a product. Once his baseball career is over, I'm positive he has a future as a game-show host.

"I don't even know how they [the fish] fit on his hook, they were so small."

DEION SANDERS, ON THE FISHING PROWESS OF TEAMMATE OTIS NIXON

CHAPTER 2

MARCH DOLDRUMS

THURSDAY, MARCH 5

The hated Dodgers were in town for that rarest of spring training animals: A Big Game.

FINALLY, THE FIRST GAME. IT'S ABOUT TIME, TOO. WATCHing grown men play catch and do stretching exercises is just about off the scale on the boring meter.

The Dodgers are here, so this is that rarest of spring-training animals: a Big Game. Atlanta and L.A. battled right down to the final weekend of the '91 season before the Braves finally clinched the NL West.

Security is very tight. How tight? One of the security guys chastised team president Stan Kasten for not wearing his pass in plain view.

Reporters are everywhere. Someone from the New York Times wants to know what Cox is going to say to his team before the game. Please.

Of course, this is nothing compared to what the TV guys are doing. Randy Waters of WXIA, Atlanta's NBC affiliate, does one report from a hot tub. Jeff Hullinger of WAGA (CBS) walks a Florida panther around the stadium. "This is not exactly Edward R. Murrow stuff," he says. True, but we all have to do a lot of stuff that hardly qualifies as hard-nosed investigative journalism, so we're not about to go pointing fingers at each other. We'll be more than happy to point fingers at each other's *editors* (and sometimes even

JOHNNY CRAWFORD

our own) for stupid assignments, but not each other.

Olson and Bream were on ABC's "Good Morning America" this morning. Olson showed weatherman Mark McEwen how to field a bunt. McEwen was wearing a huge catcher's mitt, and Olson later said, "I wanted to say to him, 'Boy, you don't need a protective cup if you use something like that,' but I didn't know if you could use the word 'cup' on television."

The game result only intensifies Bravesmania. Braves 10, Hated Dodgers 0. Justice homers. Sanders forces two pickoff errors and steals a base. Avery pitches two shutout innings. Can we go straight to the World Series? Says Dodgers manager Tommy Lasorda, "I guess the only thing we can say about this game is we won't finish the season undefeated."

David Justice lined up with his teammates for the spring opener against the Dodgers, and later hit a home run in the Braves' 10-0 win.

FRIDAY, MARCH 6

First road trip, 45 miles down I-95 to Fort Lauderdale to play the Yankees. Fort Lauderdale Stadium is old as spring parks go, but every seat is always filled. That goes for the press box, too. There's about a dozen New York guys who cover the Yankees full time, and they always move around in a pack. Today they're hot on the trail of former Braves pitcher Pascual Perez, who has disappeared from camp amid rumors he failed a drug test. A bunch of reporters jump into a car and drive off in search of Perez. Says Craig Barnes of the Fort Lauderdale *Sun-Sentinel*, who's been covering the Yankees in spring training for years, "With these guys, I feel like I'm chasing Secretariat." Later we find out that Perez did fail a drug test, and was suspended for a year.

With lunch comes an opportunity to sit in on a bull session with a couple of burly umpires, Joe West and Ken Kaiser. These guys love to tell stories. Today's topic is their most embarrassing moment. Says West, "When I came up to the majors, and this was when Candlestick Park had Astroturf, I was behind the plate and there was a ball hit deep to the fence. The ball was thrown in and actually went into the dugout. But I was watching the catcher and he made a fake tag on the runner and I called him out. The other three umpires came in and said no, no, no. Pretty embarrassing."

Kaiser recalls a game in Chicago. "I had just made this call that everybody thought was very controversial," he says. "So I'm standing at home plate between innings, and this White Sox mascot comes out there in an elephant outfit and starts getting right in my face. I picked the mascot up and threw him down hard, right on home plate. After the game, the mascot knocks on our locker-room door and wants to see me. It's a girl. And I *did* wonder why that elephant was so light."

Oh yes, the Yankees beat the Braves today, 11-6. Lasorda can relax. The Braves won't go undefeated, either.

> *"I picked the mascot up and threw him down hard, right on home plate. After the game, the mascot knocks on our locker-room door and wants to see me. It's a girl."*
>
> UMPIRE JOE WEST, ON HIS MOST EMBARRASSING MOMENT

SATURDAY, MARCH 7

Sanders comes to the ballpark with a cassette tape in his hand. It's his new rap song, with help from his buddy, Hammer. For any music historians reading this, here are the lyrics:

Saturday night, headed downstairs
The hot spot tonight, the Underground
Hugo Boss, Oh, I'm looking fine
Diamond Rolex says its Prime Time
Across the way she's dressed to impress
Like valedictorian, high above the rest.

After Sanders plays it (and everyone in the locker room goes crazy), he says it's going to be picked up by Hammer's Bustin' Records.

Come October, we'll still be waiting.

SUNDAY, MARCH 8

The clubhouse is littered with lottery tickets. The Florida lottery pot was up to $40 million, but nobody won. "Jeff [Blauser] had a press conference planned, and we were going to give him a retirement party," says Olson. Says Schuerholz, with more than a grain of truth, "Shoot, the lottery is just spending money for those players."

MONDAY, MARCH 9

The telephone call comes from Bob Hertzel of the *Pittsburgh Press*. For my money, Hertzel, who covered Cincinnati's Big Red Machine in

A spring-training ritual: Stretching, stretching and more stretching.

JOHNNY CRAWFORD

the 1970s, is one of the country's best baseball writers. He's got a tip for me, one that's going to change life as I know it for the next two weeks.

Hertzel says the Braves are interested in Pirates outfielder Barry Bonds, the 1990 NL MVP (and runner-up to Pendleton in '91). Bonds will be a free agent after this season, and everybody knows the Pirates are pinching every penny. Hertzel says Pittsburgh general manager Ted Simmons has confirmed Atlanta's interest. I've never met Simmons (he's in his first year as GM), so I call him at his spring condo, introduce myself and ask about Bonds. Simmons says he's been contacted by several clubs, including the Braves. He won't give me any more specifics, and insists a deal is not imminent.

The next call is to Schuerholz. When I bring up Bonds, the telephone goes silent. Schuerholz won't confirm or deny the report. "What Ted says, Ted says," he says. "I will not comment on any trade rumors."

Usually, if a trade rumor is wrong, Schuerholz will either laugh it off or flat deny it. The previous spring, *The National* (the short-lived all-sports daily) reported that the Braves were considering trading Justice for Oakland's Jose Canseco. When he read that one, Schuerholz called the reporter's source a liar.

That night, ESPN's Peter Gammons broaches the Bonds rumors. He says the Braves are offering Wohlers and Hunter. That doesn't make sense to me, because it wouldn't open up an outfield spot for Bonds. Yes, he's a better player than any of the current Atlanta outfielders, but the Braves aren't going to make a backup out of Justice, Gant, or both Nixon *and* Sanders (especially since they need one of those two to be the leadoff hitter). But a source inside the organization later tells me Justice may be involved in this deal, which would open up right field for Bonds.

Just how strong this outfield could be was graphically illustrated earlier in the day when Sanders went 3-for-5 with two steals in a 5-3 loss to the Mets. Sanders is being counted on to start in center field while Nixon sits out the first 18 days of the season to complete his drug suspension. Yeah, it's early, but it's beginning to look like Nixon might have some trouble getting his job back.

WEDNESDAY, MARCH 11

The clubhouse is abuzz about Bonds. Everyone's heard the rumors. Wohlers isn't happy. "I'm trying to concentrate on my pitching and making the team," he says, "and then this comes up.'

Justice is doing his best Doris Day imitation. (*Que sera, sera.*) "If I get traded," he says, "I get traded. I'll give 100 percent for whoever I play for."

Hertzel calls me back later and says super scout Bill Lajoie has been in Port Charlotte to watch Bonds play against Texas. Lajoie, former general manager of the Detroit Tigers, is Schuerholz's point man on deals. He trusts Lajoie more than anyone else in the organization.

From a money standpoint, a Bonds deal makes sense. He's likely to

Deion Sanders' early spring performance made it appear Otis Nixon might have some trouble getting his job back in center field.

be the highest-paid free agent among next year's crop, surpassing the four-year, $7.1-million-a-year deal just signed by Cubs second baseman Ryne Sandberg. Pittsburgh, one of the smallest TV markets in the majors, can't — or won't — pay him what he wants. Atlanta, with Ted Turner's cable empire and money behind the team, can.

The *Journal-Constitution's* national baseball writer, Joe Strauss, has gone to Port Charlotte to talk to Bonds. "I love Atlanta," Bonds told Strauss. "If I was in Atlanta I think I might go 30-30 [home runs and stolen bases] every year. I love Atlanta. I go there to hang out with Deion Sanders and have a great time. It's a great city. Put me in an outfield with Gant and Justice, keep guys like Glavine, Avery and Smoltz in the rotation and we'd be a dynasty."

There's no question about Bonds's talent. In '91 he hit 25 homers, drove in 116 runs and stole 43 bases, and nearly yanked the MVP award out from under Pendleton. His two-year stats of a .297 average, 199 runs scored, 58 homers, 230 RBIs and 95 stolen bases are the most complete of any NL player.

But some of the Braves are concerned about Bonds's reputation for being a troublemaker. "I'm the biggest jerk on the field," he says, "but I'm honest about it."

Before this morning's game against the Yankees in Fort Lauderdale, a 10-year-old boy came up to Cox and asked if he could interview him for a children's program. I knew this would be good; Cox hardly had patience for adult reporters. The kid asked, "Are you going to try to come back and win the World Series this year? Cox rolled his eyes. "Well," he said, "if it's all right, I think we'll try to win it again."

On the field, switch hitter Damon Berryhill homers from both sides of the plate in a 14-2 win. This team can't be stopped.

FRIDAY, MARCH 13

"Call your editor," says the message that greets me on my arrival at Chain O'Lakes Park in Winter Haven, the spring home of the Boston Red Sox. So I do.

It's about Justice. He's quoted in a long feature story in our suburban competitor, the (Gwinnett) *Daily News*, as saying, "There are a lot of good guys on this team, but there are a few who I know use the 'N' word when I'm not around."

The story, written by Braves beat writer Bill Zack, also quotes Justice as saying, "How many white players do you see get abused in the paper? We see it happen all the time with black players. When you're on the field, they love you.

"I can't tell you how many times people have looked at me when I'm off the field and because I wear a nice watch and wear good clothes, they think I'm a drug dealer."

My first move is to talk to Justice's teammates. Sanders is one of the first I approach. He immediately goes to talk to Justice, then returns. "David just said it's a bunch of bull," Sanders says.

When Justice leaves the game, I go down to the locker room to talk

WALTER STRICKLIN

A hot item around West Palm Beach: A baseball signed by every Brave you could find.

to him. He says Zack misrepresented what he said, that he never heard anybody call him a nigger behind his back, but he felt there was some racial tension on the club.

Is there? Certainly, but probably no more or no less than in society as a whole. There's nothing blatant in the clubhouse, and the players are usually unified against their two common enemies: management and the media. But guys talk behind other guys' backs, just like people do in offices and schools and factories and malls across America. Across the world.

And you couldn't force people to hang out together. As a rule, white Braves hung out with other white Braves, black Braves with other black Braves and Hispanic Braves with other Hispanic Braves. But that didn't mean the clubhouse was rife with prejudice, that there weren't genuine interracial friendships, or that the Braves were any different from any other team. From any other culturally diverse group of 40-odd males forced to take showers together.

Justice's sin, if you could call it that, was to speak honestly. Now he's concerned about how it will play.

"If this comes out and some guys on the team have a problem with it," he says, "I'll be the first to call a team meeting. I love the guys like they're my family, black or white. The thing I was saying about the media was that a lot of them have a negative focus on black players. They put a lot more attention on Pascual Perez failing a drug test than Steve Howe getting arrested with drugs.

"I'm not trying to make any big statements. I'm not trying to separate myself from the team. All I'm saying is that there is racism throughout everything and that baseball is an extension of society."

The next day, back in West Palm, Justice receives a letter and tapes it on his locker. The word "nigger" is used 13 times.

SUNDAY, MARCH 15

The Bonds deal continues to simmer. Schuerholz approaches Bream, who played with Bonds in Pittsburgh, and asks him about the All-Star outfielder. Bream admits talking to Schuerholz, but won't say what he told him about Bonds. Nixon also knows something is going on.

Later in the day, Mike Bielecki, who is being counted on as the fifth starting pitcher, is hit hard for the third straight time. His earned-run average is now at 14.85. But the day's big story is the return of two players to action. First baseman Nick Esasky hasn't played in two years because of vertigo. Catcher Mike Heath has been out since having elbow surgery last August.

MONDAY, MARCH 16

There's a new book out, called "Baseball's All-Time Goats." Writer Peter Weiss polled 300 sportswriters and broadcasters to come up with a list. It includes the obvious choices — Bill Buckner, who let a crucial ground ball go between his legs in the 1986 World Series while playing first base for the Red Sox; Ralph Branca, the Brooklyn Dodgers

> *"I love the guys like they're my family, black or white. The thing I was saying about the media was that a lot of them have a negative focus on black players."*
>
> DAVID JUSTICE, RESPONDING TO PUBLISHED REPORTS THAT HE CLAIMED THERE WAS RACIAL DISHARMONY AMONG THE BRAVES

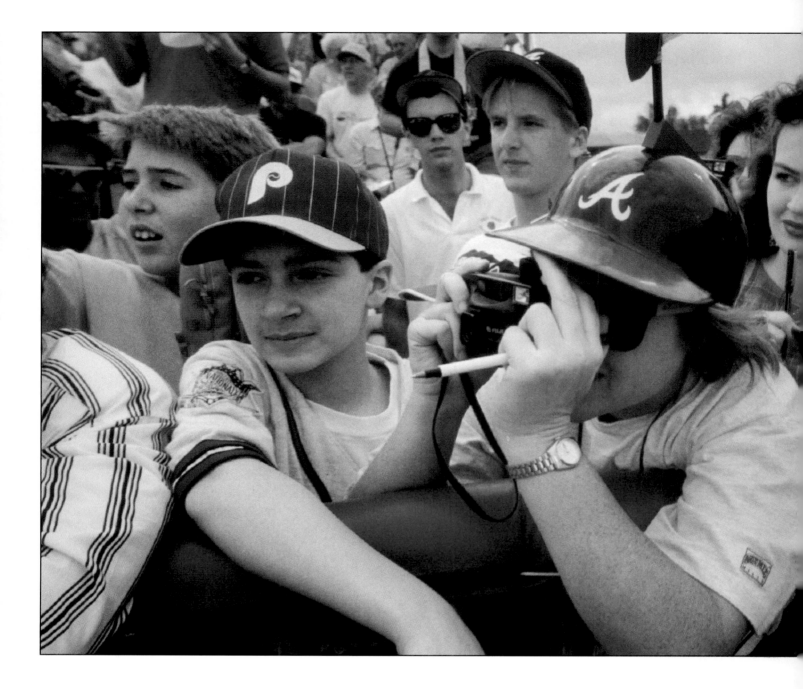

pitcher who gave up the 1951 pennant-losing home run (the "shot heard 'round the world") to the Giants' Bobby Thomson. An editor's note reads: "Lonnie Smith didn't get many votes because our survey was distributed before the '91 World Series. The few surveys that did come in after the Series, however, all nominated Smith. It will be interesting to see how history treats him."

Smith, of course, is still being skewered for his baserunning gaffe in Game 7 of the '91 Series, when he lost track of the ball on a Pendleton double and went only from first to third instead of scoring. When the Braves lost the game 1-0 in 10 innings, Smith became the goat of the Series.

Now Smith wants to be traded. He knows he's not going to get much playing time, not with Sanders looking so good. "If they have no use for me, then they can either trade me or release me," he says. Only problem is, he's 36 years old and he's got a guaranteed contract for

JOHNNY CRAWFORD

The Braves were a hit with baseball fans in West Palm Beach, with capacity crowds at almost every game at Municipal Stadium.

$1.75 million this season. No one else wants to pick it up, and the Braves don't want to eat it. So he's stuck here.

TUESDAY, MARCH 17

Ryan Klesko got sent down today. He's the top prospect in the organization, a 20-year-old, 6-foot-3, 220-pound first baseman. He's had a great spring, leading the team with a .500 average, but with Bream and Hunter ahead of him in Atlanta, he was ticketed for the top farm club in Richmond this year. "I know I didn't have much of a chance to make the team," he said, "but I thought I'd get to stick around a little longer."

I'm afraid I got Klesko into a little trouble after his demotion. I asked him to list for me the worst things about minor-league camp for a daily item our paper does called "Clubhouse Confidential." His biggest complaints were dirty sanitary socks, drinking watered-down Gatorade with no ice, standing on the field for about two hours to get in five or

WALTER STRICKLIN

The Braves came "so, so close" to adding Pittsburgh's Barry Bonds to an already crowded outfield that included David Justice and Deion Sanders.

10 minutes of work, and getting uniform clothes that look like they're washed every other day. Chuck LaMar, the club's director of scouting, was furious at Klesko's comments, and called Klesko in for a meeting with Schuerholz. Klesko said he had been misquoted. When I asked him about that, Klesko said he *had* to tell them that. Then he laughed.

WEDNESDAY, MARCH 18

Glavine missed a start and was flown back to Atlanta, where he was found to have bursitis in his left shoulder. The Braves tried to keep it quiet, but when I called Glavine's house in Atlanta, a friend who was staying there said Tommy had just been there. So I went to the airport and waited for him to get off the plane. Sure enough, there he was. He said all he needed was a fews days' rest.

The Bonds rumors were really hot. In town to talk about him were TBS president Terry McGuirk, Stan Kasten, Braves chairman of the board Bill Bartholomay and Lajoie. After a meeting, Schuerholz was given the OK to go after him. He wouldn't go on the record on the subject, but asked me what I thought. What's to think? He's the best player in baseball. Schuerholz smiled an off-the-record smile and said, "Maybe you'll be right."

THURSDAY, MARCH 19

Forget Bonds. Pittsburgh manager Jim Leyland has scotched the deal. "Under no circumstances," says Simmons, "will Barry Bonds or Doug Drabek be traded. I'm relieved, Jim Leyland is relieved. Our players are relieved. Our fans in Pittsburgh are relieved. The matter has been put to rest, period."

(A couple of months later, I was in Schuerholz's office talking about the Bonds deal. He told me, "It got so, so close; if you only knew." What it came down to was this: the Braves offered Justice, but the Pirates wanted Wohlers and Hunter. The Braves finally agreed to the deal and it was about to go through when Simmons called Schuerholz back and said Leyland didn't think he could win the division without Bonds. There was no deal.)

FRIDAY, MARCH 20

Nixon got two bouquets of roses in the clubhouse this morning. With one was a card apparently alluding to the now-dead Bonds trade negotiations. It read: "I hope you are not traded. You are my favorite player and I think you are a good person. Please call. I'm very upset."

Nixon laughed. "I love receiving flowers," he said. "I can take them home to my fiancee and tell her they're from me."

Nixon has handled his drug suspension with a lot of class. Over the winter, he agreed to break his silence about the incident that led to the drug suspension last September. Science/medicine editor Mike King and I spent several hours talking with Nixon in the furnished basement of his house at Country Club of the South, a posh golf-course community in Alpharetta, a suburb north of Atlanta. Nixon explained that he had gotten the cocaine from a pharmacist friend and tried to mask it for the drug test with salt and vinegar.

In the clubhouse, Nixon's locker was next to Sanders's, with Avery's on the other side. Nixon was constantly being asked to do interviews about the suspension, and he never failed to handle them gracefully. He also impressed me with how he dealt with another situation. One of my co-workers, Journal columnist Terence Moore, had called Nixon "a jerk" after the cocaine incident. Usually in a situation like this, the relationship between the athlete and the sportswriter was irretrievably broken, but Nixon and Moore sat in the clubhouse one day for 45 minutes and ironed out their differences.

This is just one of the many examples of why it's not easy to be an athlete or a sportswriter. Moore genuinely likes Nixon — Otis might even be his favorite person on the team — but he has no tolerance for athletes who take drugs. I know it wasn't easy for Terry to write what he did, but he remained true to his beliefs. Sometimes I'm thankful I'm not a columnist; I'm paid to keep my opinions to myself.

Nixon's in a tough position, too. When he got suspended, he was having the best season of his career and the Braves were in the thick of their division race with the Dodgers. He got savaged by media and fans. The typical media criticism was, "He's supposed to be a role

Otis Nixon was constantly being asked to do interviews about his drug suspension, and he never failed to handle them gracefully.

model for kids. How could he do that?" The typical fan criticism was, "The Braves need him to win the division. How could he do that?"

The answer, once you get past the emotionalism of the moment, is that he's human, subject to the same temptations and weaknesses as the rest of us. I can't help but wonder, when I hear people get all over his case for being addicted to cocaine, what would happen to them if the government ever outlawed their addictions. Would smokers feel morally bankrupt if they had to buy cigarettes from strangers in dark alleys? Would fat people be able to deal with random Twinkie testing?

JOEY IVANSCO

A spot along the fence that runs beside the Braves dugout was a favorite spot to try for autographs.

Today featured a rare night game — the only one, in fact, of the spring. But this one was special. It was against the Yankees at Joe Robbie Stadium, the Miami Dolphins' football home that will be adapted so the expansion Florida Marlins can use it as well.

They've got a way to go before the place is ready for major league ball. Fortunately, the Marlins don't begin play until 1993, when they'll join the Colorado Rockies in the NL. On this day, however, the turf was choppy and the bullpen mounds were in such bad shape that they couldn't be used. The pitchers had to warm up during the game on the regular mound.

The whole night was a waste. Rafael Belliard was struck in the mouth by a bad hop during batting practice and had to have eight stiches. Steve Lyons wore a catcher's mask when he went back out to third base. The game lasted more than three hours and ended in a 5-5 tie when both managers decided enough was enough. Tommy Gregg broke his left hand when he got hit by a pitch. He'll be out for the first two months of the season.

SUNDAY, MARCH 22

Halfway through the spring schedule, it's time to assess the positives and negatives (you never know when someone's going to ask for a story on that very subject). Relievers Marvin Freeman and Juan Berenguer appear to be over their injuries. Justice, Sanders and Klesko have been impressive. Pete Smith appears to be leading the competition to become the fifth starter. Bream is hitting .290. However, Bielecki, Smith's main competitor for the No. 5 starter's job, hasn't looked good, Glavine has a sore shoulder, and Olson, Berryhill and Pendleton are hitting under .200.

This morning there was a touching scene in the dugout. Justin Bentley, a 2 1/2-year-old boy from the Atlanta suburb of Acworth who was born with paralyzed vocal cords, came to the game and was given bats by Hunter, Bream, Sanders, Pendleton, Lonnie Smith and Nixon. On the field, Pete Smith finally had a bad outing, giving up seven runs on eight hits in a 9-3 loss to the Mets.

MONDAY, MARCH 23

The only day off of the spring. Most everyone went fishing or golfing. But Glavine had to test his shoulder, so he pitched for the Braves' Class A Durham, N.C., team against the Dodgers' Class A Bakersfield, Calif., farm club. He looked good, throwing four hitless innings. Of course, pitching Glavine against players from Class A, the lowest full-season level of the minor leagues, is a little like using a tank to kill a squirrel. The real point was that he pitched without pain.

THURSDAY, MARCH 26

Funny the places you get stories from. My wife, Beth Ann, was in town and met Mike Heath's wife, Linda. Linda Heath told her she had been with Pendleton's wife Catherine when she delivered a baby a few days ago. I knew the Pendletons had had a son, Terry Jr., but what I found out from Beth Ann was that Catherine had been carrying twins, but one died early in the pregnancy. I was a little surprised when Pendleton didn't hesitate to talk about the experience. He took out some pictures. "That's Terry Jr.," he said. "I would say it's the toughest thing I've been through, and now it's a big sigh of relief and serious happiness. I don't know how to explain that; it comes from within. We had known about the twin for several months. But we didn't think it was anybody else's business. I can talk about it now with people."

The baby hadn't been due until late April, so the Pendletons were caught by surprise. "We didn't have anything set up down here as far as doctors," Pendleton said. "I had to make some calls at 7 in the morning. Believe me, that was tough."

They didn't even have a name picked out yet. "It caught us by such surprise," he said, "because we weren't going to sit down with names until next month. But I thought, what better name could I give him."

Later in the day, it was back to reality, baseball-style. Pitchers David Nied, Tom McCarthy and Armando Reynoso were sent to the minor-league camp.

FRIDAY, MARCH 27

Justice is having problems with his back again. His average has dropped more than 100 points over the last week, but he's not the only one struggling. The Braves have lost five straight and haven't scored in 28 innings. Gant is hitting .179, Olson .160, Pendleton .122.

Tom Glavine had to test his shoulder. He pitched four hitless innings against the Dodgers' Class A team — a little like using a tank to kill a squirrel.

It's unusual to call a players-only meeting during spring training, but Pendleton, the club's spiritual leader, figured it was time. "I told them no matter what we did last season, we need to stop all this relaxing and lackadaisical stuff on the field," he said. "It's time to pick it up. I don't want to make a big deal about this. I just didn't like the pace we were at."

Cox isn't worried. "I'm not going to lose any sleep over it," he said. "I told them we needed to loosen up, that we didn't need for everyone to try to do too much. We need to do it as a team."

The immediate results were mixed. They lost again, 3-2 to Montreal. But at least they scored.

It's getting close to the time they have to cut the roster to the 25 players they'll take north to Atlanta, and it looks like the biggest surprise will be pitcher Ben Rivera. Not only has he never pitched in the majors, he's never even gotten to triple-A ball. He's a 23-year-old from San Pedro de Macoris, the town in the Dominican Republic that has sent so many players to the majors. He's been in the minors five years now, and he's out of options, which means that the Braves can't send him down again without making him available to other teams on the waiver wire.

Rivera is not really ready to pitch in the majors, but he has enough potential that the Braves would like to keep him. They'll probably try to hide him in middle relief, use him infrequently, hope he can develop with gradual exposure to big-league hitters.

Today's look at the minutiae of baseball concerns the errands the clubbies run for the players. Lonnie Smith has someone go to the store to get milk for his coffee. Gant always requires a pregame cheeseburger from the concession stands. Blauser and Glavine like breakfast sandwiches of bacon, eggs and cheese from a nearby deli. Smoltz is always looking for a big knife to cut his fruitcake with. It's all I can do to resist reminding him that you are what you eat.

Saturday, March 28

Some puzzle pieces are falling into place. Glavine, after pitching six scoreless innings in a 7-4 loss to the Dodgers, was named the opening-day starter. Bielecki will be the fifth starter, after Glavine, Smoltz, Avery and Leibrandt.

Wednesday, April 1

Wohlers and Keith Mitchell got sent down today. Wohlers expected it. Mitchell was upset. A 22-year-old outfielder, he got called up for 48 games last season, and hit .318 in 66 at-bats, and a lot was expected of him this spring. Unfortunately, he seemed to take the attitude that he was a lock to make the club no matter what he did, and that wasn't going to happen, not with Sanders in the picture. He was teary-eyed when he got the news. He told me it would be tough for him to go down to the minors with a good attitude. That's going to make it doubly tough for him to make it back to the majors. (He

"I told them no matter what we did last season, we need to stop all this relaxing and lackadaisical stuff on the field."

TERRY PENDLETON,
AFTER CALLING THE FIRST
PLAYERS-ONLY MEETING
OF THE YEAR

WALTER STRICKLIN

would eventually have a terrible year at Richmond and totally fall out of favor with the organization.)

There's a rumor going around that the Braves are going to take a shot at trading for San Diego catcher Benito Santiago. When he sees the item in the paper, Olson comes up to me and says, "Hey, cut that out. You're scaring my wife to death." Lisa Olson has nothing to worry about. When the season opens, Greg Olson will be the Braves' No. 1 catcher.

THURSDAY, APRIL 2

Pete Smith isn't happy. He's going to Richmond. Cox gave him the word during a brief meeting in his office that also included pitching coach Leo Mazzone. Smith hasn't pitched badly, but Bielecki beat him out for the fifth starter's job, the only spot in the rotation that was open. Their performances were pretty even, but the only way Smith was going to win the job was by being substantially better. Why? Because Schuerholz went out and traded for Bielecki at the end of last season in the deal that also brought Berryhill. In return, he sent the Cubs Atlanta's top pitching prospect, Turk Wendell. You don't trade for someone, then not use him.

Deep down, Smith understands this, but it doesn't make him feel any better. When he went to his locker after the meeting with Cox and Mazzone, Pendleton gave him a sympathetic touch on the shoulder. Jack Llewellyn, the team's sports-psychology consultant and the man given (too much?) credit for turning Smoltz's 1991 season around at the All-Star break, came over and talked to Smith for a while. When I got to Smith, though, he was still angry. "They can trade me if they want," he said, "because I think I deserve to pitch in

The practice fields are always crowded early in the spring, before the roster is slowly pared to the opening day limit of 25.

the majors."

Smith isn't the only guy upset. So is Heath. With Berryhill around, Heath never really fit into the team's plans this spring. There aren't a lot of 37-year-old third-string catchers in the majors. Schuerholz didn't want to just cut him and get no return on his investment, so he kept trying to trade him. Problem was, nobody wanted to pick up his $900,000 contract. Finally, they put him on waivers, which meant every other team had 72 hours in which to put in a claim for him. That's 72 hours during which he couldn't sign with anybody. I thought he might rip the club for waiting so long to release him, but he didn't. He merely offered this analysis of the catching situation: "I don't care what anybody says. Greg Olson isn't what this club needs. He's not that good and that should be my spot." When I relayed this to Olson for his reaction, he laughed. "Where is he now?" he asked.

FRIDAY, APRIL 3

The final day of spring training. There will be two more games — against the Cardinals in Greenville, S.C., and Little Rock, Ark. — but this is it for Florida. The final game, against the Yankees, got called early because of rain. In the clubhouse, Nixon asks me if I've heard about Sanders. I haven't heard anything, but I did notice that all his equipment was gone. Turns out he was sent back to Atlanta for a foot X-ray. He had been injured jumping into the dugout the other day. Word later comes that he has a hairline fracture. That's not good news with the opener in Houston just a few days away.

"They can trade me if they want, because I think I deserve to pitch in the majors."

PETE SMITH,
AFTER BEING ASSIGNED TO
RICHMOND AT THE END
OF SPRING TRAINING

ENCORE!

CHAPTER 3

A NEW SEASON

TUESDAY, APRIL 7

Opening day, but most of the talk in the Braves' clubhouse at the Astrodome in Houston was about Duke's win in the NCAA basketball tournament. There were a couple of NCAA pools going. Glavine won one, which had a $1,000 prize, and Leibrandt won the other, with a payout of about $500. With salaries of $2.925 million and $2.5 million apiece, they sure do need the money.

Justice is back in the lineup, his back having healed enough for him to play. But Lemke's got a pulled hamstring, and missed what would have been his first opening-day start. "I've worked so hard to get that start and now a damn injury prevents it," he said. "It sucks."

With Treadway already hurt, Blauser got the start at second. He was tired from last night, when he and teammate Steve Lyons went to see the Irish rock band U2. Lyons, a free-agent signee during the offseason, has made quite an impression on Blauser. "The guy can definitely party with the best of them," Blauser said. Around baseball, Lyons is best known as the guy who, when he was playing for the Red Sox last year, got up from a slide and pulled his pants down to clean the dirt out of them, momentarily forgetting he was doing so in

David Justice was back in the lineup opening night, his back having healed enough for him to play.

JONATHAN NEWTON

At Atlanta's home-opener, groundskeeper Ed Mangan stood on the rim above the stadium to raise the 1991 NL West championship banner.

front of a huge Fenway Park crowd and a national television audience. Lyons and Blauser got the concert tickets from an Atlanta FM radio station, 96 Rock, which wanted Blauser to do Braves reports on its morning show. But Blauser wanted more money than the station was offering, so the deal never got done. He eventually ended up doing something for WGST, the AM station that broadcasts the Braves.

Back in Atlanta, Stan Kasten was announcing that the tomahawk chop, which had been the subject of protests by Native Americans since its inception last season, would last as long as fans wanted it to last. The Braves would not give in to pressure from the Indians. Actually, the Indians kept a remarkably low profile during the offseason, after conducting a high-profile protest campaign during the playoffs and World Series. Those demonstrations apparently had been enough to convince two major publications, The Oregonian, the daily newspaper in Portland, Ore., and The Sporting News, that the use of ethnic groups as mascots was wrong. Both publications had announced that they no longer would use ethnic nicknames in print. Hence, the Braves were always referred to as "Atlanta," the Redskins as "Washington," the Indians as "Cleveland," etc.

The Braves had offered to help the Indians with some programs to educate the public about native American culture, but the Indians wanted more. They wanted the team's name changed. Kasten thought that was ridiculous, and once he got his back up about something, he was intractable. If the Indians didn't like what the Braves were offering, tough.

The opener was a roaring success. Glavine, who went in 0-8 lifetime against the Astros, struck out nine, had two hits and scored the

JONATHAN NEWTON

Brian Hunter, David Justice and their teammates got a kick out of receiving their 1991 championship rings on opening night in Atlanta.

"That really doesn't bother me. There was so much emotion out there tonight."

STEVE AVERY,
ON HIS ROUGH OUTING
IN THE HOME OPENER

JONATHAN NEWTON

ENCORE!

first run. The Braves won 2-0, their first opening-day win since 1987.

Sanders picked right up where he left off in the spring, where he finished with a .302 average. He had a double, equaling the number he had last year in 110 at-bats.

The next night, the Braves shut down the Astros 3-1 behind Smoltz. Sanders drove in a run with a single.

This doesn't look anything like the stumbling, bumbling club of spring training. Now it's time to head for Atlanta and the home opener against the San Francisco Giants.

THURSDAY, APRIL 9

There've been some big changes in the clubhouse at Atlanta-Fulton County Stadium. This is the locker room of a winner. There's a new kitchen, a players lounge with a big-screen TV and an expanded training room.

The improvements are wasted on Ron Gant, though. He hired a police officer to drive his Mercedes from West Palm to Atlanta, and she got into a wreck. "It really wasn't her fault," he said. "She was hit from behind." At least it wasn't his $200,000 Lamborghini.

Before the game, the players were presented with their diamond rings for winning the NL pennant. But they got to hold onto them for only a moment; they were collected and locked up by Casey Stevenson until after the game.

The night ended on a sour note. In front of a celebrity-studded crowd that included former president Jimmy Carter and movie star Arnold Schwarzenegger, the Braves got cuffed around by the Giants 11-4. Avery gave up two runs in the first inning — more than Glavine and Smoltz had allowed in the first two games. Afterward, after all the other reporters had left his locker, Avery admitted that maybe he was a little too excited. "That doesn't really bother me," he said, smiling. "There was so much emotion out there tonight." The loss couldn't dampen the mood in the clubhouse. Everybody couldn't wait to get back and put their rings back on. I went over to Mazzone, who had spent 23 years in the minor leagues. "This, my friend, is a dream," he said.

SUNDAY, APRIL 12

The Braves got even on Friday, when Stanton struck out Will Clark, one of baseball's most feared hitters, in the ninth with two men on base. On Saturday, however, Bielecki lost his first start as a Brave. San Francisco's Bill Swift pitched a 3-0 shutout, then had to leave because his wife was in labor. He had to catch a 10:44 flight to Seattle. He was lucky that the game took less than three hours, and he could leave for the airport at 10:05. "Police escort? I wish," he said in response to a hurried question. "It's just me and the cabbie."

(Two postscripts: He made it in time, and it was a girl.)

Glavine won the finale 6-2 for a split of the series, but there was unsettling news. Justice, who had gone 1-for-17, was complaining

The Braves came home to a remodeled clubhouse that included a new kitchen and a big-screen TV.

These Sanders pronouncements were always tough calls. Was this a legitimate, well thought-out expression of Sanders's thinking, or was he just excited about hitting .441 over the first eight games? Or more likely, was it just a negotiating ploy to try to squeeze more money out of the Falcons? Every time he came out and said, "I want to be a full-time football player," or "I want to be a full-time baseball player," you had to keep that in mind.

Of course, you also had to write virtually anything he said. If I ignored something like this on the rationalization that "it's just a cheap negotiating tactic," and our paper was the only media outlet that didn't have the story, then I'd probably wind up covering Little League. Doing "Toy Box Confidentials."

There were two things you had to give Sanders credit for. He was a hell of an athlete, and a master media manipulator. And it didn't matter that we all knew we were being manipulated. He was too hot a topic. The fans, and by extension, our editors, wouldn't let us ignore him.

So it was with mixed feelings that I wrote the story. And with more mixed feelings that I saw the headline the next day, stripped across the top of the sports front page: "Sanders says he's 'full-time' Brave." But a funny thing would happen as the season unfolded. Sanders did play the whole season with the Braves. How he did that is another story, and I don't want to get ahead of myself.

Another day, another prank. This time the victim was assistant public relations director Glen Serra. Somebody put a big silver bow and ribbon on his back, and he walked around with it for 20 minutes before noticing it.

WEDNESDAY, APRIL 15

The Reds completed the three-game sweep, winning 3-1 as the Braves managed just four hits. Yeah, it's early, but that's not good news, considering the Reds are believed to be the NL West team that most improved itself over the winter. At 4-5, the Braves fell below .500 for the first time since before the 1991 All-Star break. The Braves' only run was produced by guess who? — Sanders, on a home run, no less. He finished the series with eight hits in 10 at-bats. On the negative side, the Braves have allowed 17 stolen bases in nine games. The catchers get blamed, but this team has a bunch of pitchers who aren't especially good at holding runners on base. Half the time, the catchers have no prayer of throwing out a base-stealer. Now it's time to head for a three-game series in Los Angeles, where speedster Brett Butler has got to be salivating over those steals stats.

THURSDAY, APRIL 16

Cox decided it was time to shake up the lineup, so he started Lyons in right and Berryhill at catcher. Lyons hasn't started in so long, he doesn't even look at the lineup card anymore. He was leisurely putting on his uniform when batting instructor Clarence Jones came up to him

On their first trip to Los Angeles, the Braves lost three of four, the only win coming when Mike Bielecki beat the Dodgers 2-0 on a two-hitter.

W.A. BRIDGES JR.

THE 1992 ATLANTA BRAVES

Terry Pendleton's bat woke up during an early-season game against the Padres, when he went 3-for-4 and drove in six runs.

JONATHAN NEWTON

and wanted to go over the strengths and weaknesses of Dodgers starter Greg Gross. Lyons thought Jones was kidding. He couldn't believe it when he saw he was batting second. By game time, though, he'd recovered sufficiently to triple home the Braves' first run. On the mound, Bielecki was sharp, shutting out Los Angeles 3-0 on a two-hitter. "Bielecki was a different pitcher tonight," said Dodgers outfielder Darryl Strawberry, the former Met who remembered Bielecki from the pitcher's days with the Cubs. "He used to be a fastball and split-finger pitcher. Now he throws a lot of off-speed and keeps you off balance."

Nobody else kept the Dodgers off balance, however, as L.A. won the next three. But the spotlight remained on Sanders. Sports Illustrated sent writer Ed Hinton to Los Angeles to do a story on Sanders. As a correspondent for the magazine, I would be responsible for helping Hinton with some leg work. We knew each other anyway, because Hinton used to work for the *Journal-Constitution* before going to the National. He started writing for SI after the *National* went belly-up.

I called Sanders at the team hotel and asked him to give Hinton some time. "You saying it's SI?" he said. "No problem. You think they might put me on the cover?" Yes, they might. What was ironic about that, though, was that Hinton's story on Sanders would displace another one he'd done during spring training but hadn't run yet. One about Nixon, Sanders's best friend. Nixon was diplomatic about the news. "I just can't ever seem to beat that guy to the punch," he said.

And yes, Deion made the cover.

MONDAY, APRIL 20

San Diego Padres outfielder Tony Gwynn and I spent the better part of the afternoon talking about his new book, "Tony Gwynn's Total Baseball Player." It's an instructional book, aimed at kids, by one of the game's best hitters. After sending one of the clubbies out to his car to fetch me a copy, Gwynn asked me if I'd give the book a small plug in my paper. Maybe I'm costing myself a chance to have Robert Redford play me in the movie version of this book by admitting this, but hey, no problem, Tony. I'm not going to recommend that anybody buy it, or pass judgment on it (especially since I haven't read it), but I'll mention that it's out. Why? Because I know if I do something like this for Gwynn, he'll remember the favor and help me out when I need something. Everyone needs sources, and typically the best way to get them is to stroke a player once in a while in a harmless situation. You never know when you might get a tip on a story in return. If Redford feels like that's treasonous to the spirit of Woodward and Bernstein, well, I can live with Kevin Costner.

The Player of the Week award is out, and unbelievably, Sanders didn't get it, despite hitting .500 (14-for-28) with four triples. Unbelievable, that it, unless you understand how these awards are decided. They're given out by the league office, which means a couple of anonymous people look at the players who were nominated and come to a consensus. There's an unwritten rule not to give the award

Unbelievably, Deion Sanders didn't get the Player of the Week award, despite hitting .500 (14-for-28) with four triples.

JONATHAN NEWTON

to teammates in consecutive weeks, so that's why Dodgers pitcher Tom Candiotti won it this time despite giving up two runs in each of his wins. Because Glavine won the award last week.

The Padres proved to be just what the Braves needed. They cruised 10-4 in the opener, as Pendleton had six RBIs. "I just hope it's a good omen," he said. It wasn't. The next night, not only did the Braves lose, but Sanders saw his 14-game hitting streak ended and his average dip below .400 for the first time in nine days. There also was a lesson in baseball superstition and jealousy. Avery, who had been rubbing Sanders's bats for luck, had been bragging that he was responsible for the hitting streak. But what he didn't know was that Sanders, on the sly, had asked Mercker to rub his bats. Mercker had screwed up, though, and mistakenly rubbed Pendleton's bats. That was the day Pendleton went 3-for-4 and drove in six runs. When Mercker learned of his fortuitous mistake, he crowed, "Take that, Avery."

The Braves also lost the series finale 9-4. That gave them some pretty ugly stats for the road trip, which was now over. They went 2-8, were outscored 45-39, and had more strikeouts (78) than hits (76). Glavine, Smoltz and Avery lost all six of the games they started.

Lonnie Smith exemplified the players' frustrations when he was tossed out of the finale for arguing a third-strike call. Smith cursed,

April 24: For the first time in seven months, Otis Nixon was on the field for a regular-season game.

spat, and tried to get in umpire Jim Quick's face. He had to be restrained by Cox and three coaches.

The plane ride home to Atlanta was much calmer. They weren't happy about being 6-10, but they weren't even a tenth of the way through the season.

FRIDAY, APRIL 24

Nixon is back. His drug suspension has been served. He and Sanders will be in the lineup until Justice comes off the disabled list. Nixon sat at his locker and talked about how tough it was sitting out.

"Sort of strange," he said. "I've been waiting for this day a long time. Ever since I was sitting in that drug rehab center I started thinking about it. That was a time when I was really hurting, even crying some. I think that surprised me more than anything that I could open up like that. But a lot of things have changed. You'll see."

Since this was a home game, the first of nine in a row, everyone wondered what sort of reception Nixon would get when he was announced to the crowd. After all, a lot of people dumped a lot of abuse on him when he was suspended.

As it turned out, Nixon had been forgiven. The few catcalls from the stands were drowned out by the overwhelming majority of cheers, and many stood as they applauded.

"That was a relief, to be honest with you," Nixon said later. "I wasn't exactly sure how that would go. Now that I know they're behind me in the city, it doesn't matter what happens when I leave to play on the road."

It also was a relief for Schuerholz.

"The vitriolic letter writers and screamers weren't here," he said. "They were probably sitting at home in a room by themselves with the game on TV, not wanting anybody to know they were watching. I don't mean to be smart-alecky about this, I understand people have real concerns about this issue. But I also understand that there's still an element of compassion available to people."

Compassion, yes. Competence, no. The Astros beat Atlanta 4-2.

SATURDAY, APRIL 25

Finally, a win. Avery shut out the Astros 2-0, and Bream got his first RBI of the season after going 0-for-9 with runners in scoring position.

A lot of fans have been asking why Cox didn't move Justice to first base when he returned to the lineup, and thus be able to play both Nixon and Sanders in the outfield. Privately, Cox said he considered the move, but ultimately decided to be patient with Bream and Hunter. Justice has played some first base (he played 69 games there in 1990 when Esasky went down with vertigo), but he isn't a first baseman. And Cox has never been one to make rash decisions.

On Sunday, another win. The Braves had their first back-to-back victories since the first two days of the season.

A children's group wowed the crowd with its rendition of the national anthem before a game against the Expos.

MARLENE KARAS

ENCORE!

JONATHAN NEWTON

MONDAY, APRIL 27

Blauser was irked. Miffed, even. The paper runs a daily item in which it answers readers' questions about the club. Someone had asked sarcastically, "Has Jeff Blauser ever been successful stealing a base?" The answer, written by one of my editors, was "Blauser, no gazelle, has stolen 21 bases in his career." Blauser called me back to his locker and wanted to know what "this gazelle" stuff was. "You look around the room and see a lot of guys that haven't stolen as many bases as me," he said. He was right. Bream had only 15 career stolen bases, Olson two and Lemke one. There were a lot of non-gazelles on the roster.

But Blauser's beef was small potatoes compared to what Lyons was going through. Cox told him he was going to be assigned to a minor-league team. Lyons was furious, feeling he never had a chance to prove himself. "It makes me wonder why they signed me at all," he said. They undoubtedly were wondering the same thing when they had to eat his $600,000 contract after they released him. "I didn't give him a good shot at playing," Cox admitted, "but who would have thought Deion would hit .400?"

No gazelle? Jeff Blauser was offended by a joke about his speed — or the supposed lack of it.

ENCORE!

CHAPTER 4

FROM FIRST TO WORST?

TUESDAY, APRIL 28

SANDERS MAY HAVE A NIKE DEAL IN THE WORKS. WHEN I asked if he was going to replace Bo Jackson as the shoe company's major spokesman, he just winked. Nike wasn't terribly forthcoming with specifics, but I found out the key to getting the deal done was the clause in the contract specifying how much Sanders would make under each of three scenarios: just play baseball, just play football, or just play both. The early word is that it's $1 million a year for both, $100,000 for either one.

Dusty Kidd, Nike's public relations director, wouldn't bite at my attempts to get him to compare Sanders and Jackson. "It would be dangerous to compare any athlete with Bo Jackson," he said. (Dangerous? You mean like, fearing for your own safety?) "It's sort of like Michael Jordan and Scottie Pippen. One is vastly more recognized than the other. Every athlete has their own identity." Well, gee, thanks, Dusty, and feel free to kick me the next time I try to get quotes out of a PR guy.

While the public Sanders is engaged in endorsement deals, the private one has other priorities. He's been all over me about Moore and his columns. He seems to

The key to Deion Sanders's Nike deal was the clause concerning whether he played baseball, football or both.

JONATHAN NEWTON

innings streak is up to 33 now, a franchise record. In the three wins over the Cubs, the Braves held Chicago batters to 12 hits, a .132 average, and struck out 21 while walking only four. At 11-11, the Braves reached the .500 mark for the first time since Week 1 of the season.

It was also announced that ticket sales had reached 1 million, but neither that nor the three shutouts were the big topic of conversation in the clubhouse. That was the appearance of two short-skirted Scottish journalists. Considering that Scottish men wear kilts, I guess I need to specify that these were women. Certainly every male in the locker room noticed that they were women. The only thing that got most of the players to stop staring was an attempt by a disc jockey from a local FM station, Z-93, to approach Justice. Bad move. First, Justice has a show on a competing station, Star 94. Plus, he wasn't happy with Z-93 for saying he was dating a centerfold. (He wasn't.) Justice, however, handled himself well. "Z-93 is the reason I'm not hitting," he said. "Don't listen to them."

A DJ from Z-93 tried to approach David Justice in the locker room. Bad move. First, Justice had a show on a competing station, Star 94. Plus, he wasn't happy with Z-93 for saying he was dating a centerfold. (He wasn't.)

FRIDAY, MAY 1

The crowd was only 31,637 to see the Mets come to town, down considerable from the expected 40,000-plus. A lot of people apparently didn't want to come downtown only 24 hours after civil disturbances in the wake of the Rodney King riots in L.A. The Braves had offered tickets to other games for anyone who didn't want to come to this game. Those who chose to stay away missed a heck of a game.

RICH MAHAN

Tom Glavine beat the Mets 3-0, pitching his second straight shutout and raising his record to 4-1.

The Braves rallied from a 7-1 deficit with a six-run seventh, but lost 8-7 on an eighth-inning homer by Darryl Boston.

The next night, Glavine pitched his second straight shutout, winning 3-0 and raising his record to 4-1. After the game, Lemke had public relations director Jim Schultz call official scorer Mark Frederickson after the game to ask why Lemke wasn't given a hit when pitcher Anthony Young failed to field a slow roller in front of the mound. When Frederickson came down to the clubhouse and approached Lemke, the second baseman acted as if he didn't know what was going on. "I really didn't want to make a big deal about it," Lemke said later. Said Frederickson, "I have no problem with coming down here and seeing what they want. The problem is they usually will never say anything. The thing that some people don't realize is that we also make mistakes."

THE 1992 ATLANTA BRAVES

61

Yeah, I get that all the time, too. Nobody ever seems to realize that I make a mistake from time to time, too.

MONDAY, MAY 4

Sometimes I think these guys have too much time on their hands. Avery and Smoltz decided to alter their teammates' names above their lockers by erasing letters selectively. For Jerry Willard, they spelled out LARD. For Pendelton they spelled out PEON. For Blauser, LUSER. For Belliard, they got LIAR. And for Smoltz, Avery erased the top part of the O and made it read SMUT.

TUESDAY, MAY 5

A word about card shows. Just as baseball employs a Type A, Type B and Type C ranking system for players' on-field performance, promoters have a similar scale for who makes what on the autograph circuit. For instance, for a three-hour session, Justice would be paid about $15,000. Other players in that group would include Seattle's Ken Griffey Jr. and Chicago White Sox first baseman Frank Thomas. The next group, which would get $5,000-$10,000, would include such players as Avery, Glavine and Gant. The Olsons, Blausers, etc. would get $2,000-$5,000.

I went to talk to bullpen coach Ned Yost and noticed a folder in his locker with all his street clothes listed on it. Turns out Yost dresses by the numbers. With the help of an Atlanta clothier, he always knew which pair of pants to wear with which coat and which tie to wear with which shirt. Each item was numbered, and all the number combinations were listed in the folder. "This just makes it very easy for me," he said, "and before it wasn't." Sanders wasn't about to pass up a chance to needle him. "Hey, Ned," he said, "when you're ready to step out of coaching clothes and into some of ours, look me up in the yellow pages."

Hey, at least Yost was wearing something unique. Pendleton and Nixon showed up wearing the same suit, a teal Hugo Boss double-breasted jacket with pleated pants. "At least I know I'm in good company," said Nixon.

WEDNESDAY, MAY 6

What was the name of that movie about the Titanic? "A Night to Remember"? The Braves were leading the Pirates 3-2 in the bottom of the 13th inning at Three Rivers Stadium, their first meeting since last year's playoffs. With runners at first and second and two out, Pittsburgh's Jay Bell lofted a fly ball into short right field. Lemke drifted back. Justice drifted in. Fans drifted toward the exits. Pittsburgh manager Jim Leyland turned and headed for the tunnel leading from the dugout to the clubhouse. But wait! The ball fell in and the tying run came home. The Pirates went on to win 4-3 in 16 innings.

But this wasn't just another loss. After the miscommunication on the field, Lemke tried to approach Justice in the dugout. Justice threw

Mark Lemke and David Justice feuded over who was to blame for a dropped pop-up that led to a 16-inning loss to the Pirates.

up his hands and walked into the tunnel. The scene was captured on TV for however many fans were still awake. The only break the Braves got was that the game was being shown by SportSouth, not WTBS, so it was only a regional broadcast and not a national one.

The next day, both players put on their best public faces. Lemke took the blame, and Justice said, "We practically grew up together. I still love Mark like I always loved Mark."

Privately, however, Lemke told me he was sick and tired of Justice's selfishness. It bothered him that Justice was letting him take the whole rap. It would continue to bother him for several days, but he never took Justice aside to try to straighten things out. Eventually, the incident was forgotten.

SATURDAY, MAY 9

Another day, another movie title. How about "Beat Me in St. Louis"? Or, for Spike Lee fans, "Mo Bullpen Blues." Actually, I have to credit our national baseball guy, Joe Strauss, for that. Some editor who probably doesn't even know who Spike Lee is took that out of his copy one time, and I promised him I'd get it into the book. It's perfect. The Braves blew a 9-0 lead when the bullpen allowed five runs. The final score was 12-11, with the winning run scored by another two-sport athlete, Brian Jordan. Jordan played last football season in the same Falcons defensive backfield as Sanders, but he decided to quit football to pursue baseball full time. Smoltz, the starter and loser, was furious afterward, but he wasn't exactly standing on the firmest of cases. He did, after all, give up seven runs in 6 2/3 innings.

The next day, it happened again. The Braves were leading 5-2 in the seventh but lost 6-5. Peña blew the save and took the loss. Shades of the Ghastly Boys, a Strauss term from 1990 that played off the Reds' formidable corps of relievers, the Nasty Boys. In all four losses on this road trip, the Braves had given away the lead in either the eighth or ninth innings. Peña had allowed five earned runs in his last three appearances. Stanton lasted only one out in the 6-5 loss, and his ERA was an ugly 5.40. Berenguer allowed four runs and managed just three outs in his last three performances.

Before Sunday's game, umpire Bruce Froemming had a great story. Fellow umpire Ed Montague told him they could get $250,000 from a Japanese group to run an umpiring clinic in Japan for a month. So a meeting was arranged, and Froemming, Montague and several Japanese went to lunch in Philadelphia. "I even drank sake," said Froemming. "It tasted like bird sweat, but for $250,000 I'd drink anything." The Japanese told him his $500 advance would be arriving soon, but Froemming thought he was getting $50,000. One of the Japanese said, "That's 50,000 yen." Soon after, former ballplayer and all-time prankster Jay Johnstone showed up, decked out in traditional Japanese attire. Said Froemming, "Montague will get his. There are two words — get even — and I will get even."

W. A. BRIDGES JR.

The Braves and their bullpen were struggling. Alejandro Peña had allowed five runs in his last three appearances.

WEDNESDAY, MAY 13

Back in Atlanta, Bonds and Sanders were standing around the batting cage underneath the stadium. Theirs is a fairly typical sports relationship, where initial respect for each other's talent has become the basis of a friendship. Bonds was talking about his high school days in San Mateo, Calif., when he played football.

"Everybody offered me a scholarship in football," he said. "I had a lot more offers than baseball scholarships. But once I saw somebody get hurt badly, that was all I needed to see." Bonds recalled his first experience with organized football, during his sophomore year of high school.

"I had never played anything but mud football," he said. "The first thing I was given was pads and pants. I put on the pants and thought you taped the pads on the outside. And I had no idea of what to do with the shoulder pads."

Bonds had come to Atlanta over the winter to play in Sanders's charity basketball game. "The biggest thing that ever happened to me was beating Deion in the slam-fest," he said. "Shoot," said Sanders, "he comes up there and bounces the ball perfectly and then makes the slam and everybody goes crazy. The reason he did it was because of the way he bounced it. If he had missed it, that ball still would have gone in the net."

FRIDAY, MAY 15

Mercker wanted to talk. He was frustrated that Cox wasn't using him. I told him Cox had two beefs with him: wildness and a propensity to give up home runs. I also told him that Cox just seems to trust Stanton more, although surely Mercker could see that for himself. As upset as Mercker was, he wouldn't go to Cox himself. Maybe he wanted me to do it in print, but it isn't within a beat reporter's province to make suggestions to a manager. A columnist can do it, though, and the next day the headline on Mark Bradley's column was "Mercker's left arm could save the Braves." But the next night brought a 7-1 loss to Montreal in which Peña continued to struggle, giving up two home runs, and Mercker remained on the bench.

Another unhappy player was Nixon, who didn't like having to platoon with Sanders in center field. "I'd like to see Deion and myself in there at the same time," he said. "Right now it's tough because we're hitting so well. When it's going like that, you should be in there every day." It was tough to argue with their numbers. Nixon was hitting .406, Sanders .328.

Justice was stuck in the slow lane at .167, but Cox kept him in the lineup, even in the face of mounting fan criticism. Cox, whose ability to keep his players happy was regarded as his biggest strength as a manager, felt that taking Justice out of the lineup would destroy his confidence. Publicly, he said, "Scoring has not been our problem." Nixon said he planned to sit down with Cox in a couple of days and discuss the situation.

"The biggest thing that ever happened to me was beating Deion in the slam-fest."

BARRY BONDS,
ON HIS OFF-SEASON TRIP
TO ATLANTA
TO PLAY IN DEION
SANDERS'S CHARITY
BASKETBALL GAME

FRANK NIEMEIR

MONDAY, MAY 18

Open warfare has been declared. Somebody in the stands hit Justice with a handful of peanuts. Got him right in the on-deck circle during a 5-1 win over the Cardinals. "It's no fun playing at home," he said afterward. "You don't see that in St. Louis. You don't see that in Chicago. I'm not saying that every fan is like that. We have a lot of loyal fans. ... Just keep the rest of them out." He felt the media was partially to blame for his problems with fans. "It's this image they have about me, created by what they read about me," he said. "I knew it would happen."

There's never an excuse for throwing something at a player, but judging by other players' stories about things that had been thrown at them, Justice was fortunate it was only peanuts. Nixon said that when he was playing for Cleveland, a fan in Detroit threw a $500 pair of binoculars at him. (I guess the price tag was still on them, I don't know.) He said he gave them to the groundskeeper and got them back after the inning. Peña said he was once hit on the head by an apple. Cox said when he was in Venezuela, a snake was thrown at him.

The record was 18-22, not what anybody expected. The players had their first meeting of the season, called by Pendleton and Bream. Bream did most of the talking. "They made it very simple," Blauser said afterward. "They told us to get out asses in gear."

"I'd like to see Deion and myself in there at the same time. It's tough because we're hitting so well. When it's going like that, you should be in there every day."

OTIS NIXON,
WHO WAS UNHAPPY
TO BE RIDING THE BENCH
DESPITE A .406 AVERAGE.

"It's no fun playing at home. ... I'm not saying that every fan is like that. We have a lot of loyal fans. Just keep the rest of them out."

DAVID JUSTICE,
AFTER BEING PELTED
WITH PEANUTS IN
THE ON-DECK CIRCLE.

FRANK NIEMEIR

ENCORE!

THE 1992 ATLANTA BRAVES

WEDNESDAY, MAY 20

Nixon went fishing this morning, but he's the one who almost got caught. His development, Country Club of the South, is overwhelmingly white. He got up early to fish in a stream that borders the property. To get there, he had to climb a 10-foot-high fence topped with barbed wire. After he jumped the fence, a woman came jogging past with her dog. He startled her, and she ran off to find the security people. Nixon, meanwhile, rigged his pole and began to fish. A couple of minutes later, Nixon was surrounded by security guards, but once they recognized him, they all had a good laugh. I'm not so sure I would have laughed if I were Nixon, but he's about as easy going a person as I've ever met.

Segregation isn't limited to exclusive housing developments. Even the Braves' clubhouse breaks down along racial lines in the cliques that have formed. Among the blacks, Justice hangs out with Hunter, Gant and Sanders. Sanders doesn't spend as much time with Avery as he used to. Nixon and Sanders hang out together, but Nixon generally avoids Justice. There's a white card-players' group that includes Olson, Leibrandt, Avery and Smoltz. The Hispanics — Belliard, Peña and Berenguer — stick together. Surprisingly, one of the loners is Pendleton, perhaps because he feels it would detract from his position of leadership to affiliate himself with any one clique. He spends most of his time in the training room getting his hamstrings treated or on the telephone with his family. Lonnie Smith keeps to himself, talking mainly to the batboys. Freeman is also a loner. Back in the corner is Blauser's territory, where he and Lemke spend most of their time around Blauser's locker, which includes a lot of pictures of naked women and a life-size poster of Olson (clothed). There's also a little male doll. When you squeeze an attached bulb, its pants come down.

FRIDAY, MAY 22

A nine-game road trip began today in Montreal, with stops ahead in Philadelphia and New York. No. 3 catcher Jerry Willard was telling me about his 11 years in the minors. He has two favorite stories. "I was playing at Class A Reading (Pa.) and we had gotten up before dawn to take a six-hour bus ride," he said. "Everyone was trying to find a comfortable way to sleep. One guy laid in the chair and put his feet up in the air. When he was sleeping, someone tied his shoelaces to the wire that runs along the window, and he was stuck in that position. It was great. When he woke up he couldn't move.

"Another was when we were taking a bus ride and these two guys lost all their money, including what they got for meals, in a card game. So they borrowed $5 and went out and bought a big jar of peanut butter, jam and bread. That's what they ate for six days."

The Expos fired manager Tom Runnells and hired former Brave Felipe Alou, who becomes the first Dominican to manage in the majors. The Expos gave Alou a 7-1 victory as a present in his first game, as Dennis Martinez knocked off Glavine.

One of the loners in the clubhouse is Terry Pendleton, perhaps because he feels it would detract from his position of leadership to affiliate himself with any one clique.

JONATHAN NEWTON

SUNDAY, MAY 24

Smoltz struck out a career-high and Atlanta-record 15 batters today as the Braves beat the Expos 2-1. "After you face a guy like that," said Montreal's Larry Walker, "you come straight to your locker, throw your clothes off, take a shower and go home. There was nothing anybody was going to do." Smoltz struck out the final Expo batter, Gary Carter, for his 15th K, which tied the Braves record set by Warren Spahn on Sept. 16, 1960, in Milwaukee. The 15 strikeouts also were four more than Smoltz's previous best.

The most memorable part of the day, though, was another practical joke, again at the expense of Lovell. Just before the plane was to take off for Philadelphia, he discovered his shoes had been stolen and replaced with a pair of green, platform-soled jobs that looked like they came right out of John Travolta's closet. There's a dress code on these flights that prohibits wearing sneakers, so he had to wear these abominations. If you figure he took a lot of grief, you're right.

MONDAY, MAY 25

A trip to Philadelphia means a chance to talk to the Phillies' John Kruk, one of the most entertaining players in the league. With a physique that resembles Babe Ruth's, he once was described by Braves TV analyst Don Sutton as looking "like a guy who went to a fantasy

"After you face a guy like that, you come straight to your locker, throw your clothes off, take a shower and go home. There was nothing anybody was going to do."

MONTREAL'S
LARRY WALKER, AFTER
JOHN SMOLTZ STRUCK
OUT 15 EXPOS

camp and stayed." He says George Wendt (Norm on the TV show "Cheers") will play him in the film version of his life. In his spare time, he waches professional wrestling and Foghorn Leghorn cartoons. He says he can't imagine himself with a real job, working for a living. Neither can I.

TUESDAY, MAY 26

Rock bottom. A 5-2 loss to the Phillies drops the Braves into last place with a 20-27 record. They've scored just one run without the aid of an error in their last 26 innings. They've gone down in order in 10 of their last 18 innings.

But nobody's panicking. It's still early. (How early? My editors haven't yet asked for the first "if-the-season-ended-today" story.)

FRANK NEIMEIR

The day after a loss to the Phillies dropped the Braves into last place, Bobby Cox shook up his lineup. The Braves won 9-3.

One of the calmer voices belongs to Sutton, who stresses that there's nothing to be concerned about. Sutton is one of the most respected announcers around, having risen beyond the level attained by most ex-jocks. When you've won more than 300 games in the majors, people tend to listen to you, but they'll stop pretty fast if you don't have anything worthwhile to say. Sutton also has one of the best treasure troves of baseball anecdotes, most of them from his days with the Dodgers and manager Tommy Lasorda, his constant nemesis.

They rarely got along. One time in Pittsburgh, Lasorda pinch-hit for Sutton in the sixth inning of a game where the Dodgers trailed 1-0. There was one out and no one on base, and Sutton didn't feel like he should be taken out. "Everyone in the dugout was waiting for me to tear something up or throw something," he said. "But I put on my jacket, went to the clubhouse, changed my shoes and went up to the Allegheny Club [the Pirates' stadium club, with windows overlooking the field]. I was wearing my uniform and Dodgers jacket and got a table by the window, ordered dinner and a bottle of wine (charged, of course, to the Dodgers) and called down to the dugout."

Rick Sutcliffe picked up the phone, and Sutton told him to get Red Adams, the pitching coach. Adams asked who it was, and Sutcliffe said it was Sutton. Adams asked, "Where is he?" Sutcliffe pointed up toward the club, and suddenly all heads shifted in that direction, including Lasorda's.

"I then saw Tommy get up and starting cussing up and down," Sutton said, laughing at the memory. "Hey, the rule was you couldn't leave the ballpark until after the game was over. I didn't leave."

The next day Cox shook up his lineup, benching Justice. The Braves won 9-3. Afterward, basketball player Charles Barkley of the Philadelphia 76ers visited the clubhouse.

"You see," he said, "I bring you boys luck."

He was right. He just didn't know how right.

CHAPTER 5

YOUNG GUNS RIDE AGAIN

SUNDAY, MAY 31

It WAS TWO HOURS BEFORE THE SCHEDULED FIRST PITCH at Shea Stadium, but the pouring rain made it obvious there would be no game today. That was disappointing to the Braves, for after three straight wins, they were eager to keep playing.

"I think maybe we gained a little hope in ourselves and put a little hope back in the people of Atlanta," said Bream.

The Ben Rivera experiment is over. On Thursday, Schuerholz traded the pitcher to the Philadelphia Phillies for pitcher Donnie Elliott. Schuerholz didn't like to give up on Rivera, but he knew the bullpen needed help, and he had to clear a spot on the roster to bring up Wohlers.

Since Rivera couldn't be sent to the minors without being waived — and certainly without being claimed by someone — Schuerholz got what he could for him in a trade. Elliott will be of no immediate help — he was sent to Greenville — but at least Schuerholz got something in return.

> "I think maybe we gained a little hope in ourselves and put a little hope back in the people of Atlanta."
>
> SID BREAM,
> ON THE BRAVES' THREE-GAME WINNING STREAK SINCE FALLING INTO LAST PLACE

On Saturday, Schuerholz made another pitching move, placing Freeman on the 15-day disabled list with tendinitis in his right shoulder and calling up Pete Smith from Richmond.

But the immediate concern on Sunday, once the game was called off, was to get home without waiting for the charter, which wouldn't arrive until early evening. There was a flight to Atlanta leaving in 30 minutes, but getting from Shea Stadium to the airport in less than a half-hour is a neat trick. It's not that far away; but getting anywhere in New York in less than a half-hour is a neat trick. Sutton, however, had the solution. He went into the police precinct at the stadium and talked one of the cops into taking us to the airport in a police van. "Don is the best at this," said his announcing partner, Skip Caray. "But you had to wonder what they were thinking at Delta when they see us getting out of a police van."

RICH MAHAN

We had to get to the airport in 30 minutes. Don Sutton had the solution. He went into the police precinct at the stadium and talked one of the cops into taking us to the airport in a police van.

FRIDAY, JUNE 5

San Diego. What better place than the laid-back capital of America to sit back during an early-afternoon visit to the clubhouse and compose a few thoughts on the relationships these players have with the media and with each other. So let's go once around the locker room:

Blauser: A very popular guy, a class-clown type whose act relies heavily on imitations of bodily functions.

Berryhill: Pretty much a loner who spends a lot of time watching television in the players' lounge. He makes no waves, and seems to have no enemies.

Justice: Another loner, although he is close to Hunter. Very suspicious of the media, which is understandable considering his propensity for sounding self-serving whenever he does talk. He's almost always the last one to arrive at the park. He's one of the mainstays of this team, and it hinders me that I seem to be in his doghouse. But I'm hardly the only reporter or player who's in there, and I'm not going to suck up to him. I make it a point, though, to repeatedly consult my editors about whether I'm being fair to the guy in my copy. So far, they haven't had any complaints.

Hunter: Quiet, spends a lot of time reading newspapers and magazines. He's Justice's biggest buddy, and gets a kick out of calling me names. I would not describe him as mature, but in fairness, neither would I use that term in connection with a lot of other guys on this team.

A brief timeout here for a quick lesson in relationships between reporters and athletes, and reporters and fans. There are always going to be players who don't like you, who feel you've treated them unfairly. You disagree. You think their concept of fairness is for you never to write anything about them that isn't glowingly positive. The ground rules are, you don't have to like each other, you don't have to talk to each other. But both sides have an obligation not to be abusive to each other. I don't abuse Justice or Hunter, either in print or in person, and I expect them to treat me the same way. If they've got a problem with

Clubhouse manners: Brian Hunter is quiet, and spends a lot of time reading newspapers and magazines. He's David Justice's biggest buddy.

JONATHAN NEWTON

Marvin Freeman is loud and boisterous when he does well, stone silent when he doesn't. He can be one of the funniest guys on the team, though, and it's impossible not to like him.

FRANK NIEMEIR

ENCORE!

something I write, I'll be delighted to discuss it.

Now for the fans. I'm certain there will be people who read this and say, "I knew Rosenberg hates Justice. That's why he writes all that bad stuff about him." Well, Mr. or Mrs. Fan, that's just not the way it is. I write about what happens. If Justice isn't hitting, I write about it. If his relationship with his teammates is affecting the club, I write about it. If he's getting roasted on the talk shows about his back injury, I write about it. But if he hits a home run, I write about that, too. If he appears on a soap opera, I write about that. If he rescues a little kid from a burning building, I write about that.

If you ask me if I like the guy, I'd have to say no. I doubt you would, either, if you were in my shoes. But as long as I don't let my feelings affect what I write, there's nothing wrong with that. The problem comes when fans don't read very carefully. Say I write that the Braves are considering trading Justice for Bonds. Our paper will get calls from people who say they're upset because I'm trying to get rid of Justice. That's bull. Someone argued with one of my editors once that I was trying to influence the Braves to make that move by writing about it. If anyone thinks I can influence Schuerholz to do anything, well, I've got some land down in Florida I can let you have cheap.

But it's time to get off the soap box and back into the clubhouse. Who's next?

Pendleton: He's the team leader, even though he's rarely at his locker. Most of the time he's in the training room or talking to his wife on the phone. But he never blows anybody off and his teammates respect him tremendously.

Smoltz: One of the card players. When he isn't shuffling or dealing, he likes to talk about golf, at which he is very good. He also won't hesitate to tell me when something I write bothers him, but in a calm, rational manner. He also gets media brownie points for always giving a considered, thoughtful answer to any question. Unlike a lot of his teammates, he never starts an answer by insulting the question.

Glavine: Well respected by almost everyone on the team. He's the club's representative to the players' union.

Bielecki: One of the nicest guys on the team. Always makes time to talk.

Mercker: Loves to voice his complaints to the media. Maybe that's why he's never been one of Cox's favorites.

Freeman: In fairly typical athlete fashion, he's loud and boisterous when he does well, stone silent when he doesn't. He can be one of the funniest guys on the team, though, and it's impossible not to like him.

Peña: The ultimate loner. Very tough to interview, although not overtly unfriendly.

Lemke: A lot of the offseason attention that followed his World Series heroics seemed to go to his head, but he warmed up again quickly. A jokester in the Blauser mold.

Stanton: Doesn't like criticism, which makes him a tough inter-

If anyone thinks I can influence John Schuerholz to do anything, well, I've got some land down in Florida I can let you have cheap.

view when he blows a save.

Gant: A dichotomy. Doesn't feel as if he gets the media attention he deserves, but seems to hate talking to reporters. Even after getting a game-winning hit, he'll take forever to come out of the shower.

Sanders: At the beginning of the year he was a pleasure to deal with. But the more attention he got, the more difficult he became. His celebrated friendship with Avery seemed to dissolve as he began spending more time with Justice.

Avery: One of the team's biggest pranksters, and he also has been dragged into the card clique. Like Smoltz and Glavine, he has learned how to deal with the media, and he always talks, even after the worst performances.

Lonnie Smith: Spends most of his time talking to the batboys and smoking cigarettes. He also has gotten involved with the card games. Often stonewalls the media when his performance is questioned, but sometimes can be very engaging

Nixon: Loves electronic gadgets. Has a cellular phone, an electronic calendar and a laptop computer, in which he stores a lot of his information on opposing pitchers and their pickoff moves.

Olson: The club's biggest media hound. Maybe it's because he spent eight years in the minors, but he'll do anything for a buck and some attention. But he's also a genuinely nice guy, always good for a quote.

Leibrandt: Another one who seems to like to keep the media waiting after a game. His postgame ritual is a shower and shave, which means it's at least 20 minutes before he makes his way out of the shower. Overall, though, a class act.

Bream: Runs the team's religious services. Actually answers mail from fans. The thing I like most about him is that he always gives you a straight answer to a question.

Treadway: Popular even though he doesn't spend much time hanging around with his teammates. A frequent guest in Cox's doghouse.

Berenguer: A frequent complainer, which isn't unusual for a closer, whose performance is usually judged by the last batter he faced.

Belliard: A wonderful disposition, though it's tough to get close to him without speaking Spanish, something I don't do very well.

Wohlers: Still just a kid, and hasn't really found a niche yet.

In the opener against the Padres, the Braves trailed 2-1 in the ninth, but Blauser tied it on a homer. They then loaded the bases with one out, and scored the winning run when Olson drew a walk.

Wohlers came on for his second save, but it wasn't easy. He walked Jerald Clark to lead off the bottom of the ninth, and gave up a bunt single to Kurt Stillwell. Oscar Azocar sacrificed the runners to second and third, but Tony Fernandez slapped a grounder back to Wohlers, and Clark was caught in a rundown between third and home. Tony Gwynn, the league's second-leading hitter, was walked to load the bases, but Gary Sheffield grounded into a game-ending force play.

Otis Nixon loves electronic gadgets. He has a cellular phone, an electronic calendar and a laptop computer, in which he stores information on opposing pitchers and their pickoff moves.

"That is probably as tough a lineup as there is in baseball right now," said Cox. "And walking Gwynn to get to a guy like Sheffield is like shooting your foot full of bullets."

The road trip was off to a positive start, an unexpected start for a team 12-17 away from home. Back East, Esasky has finally decided to go to Richmond for his rehabilitation assignment. In his first game for the R-Braves, he hit a home run.

SUNDAY, JUNE 7

A 9-4 win that completed the three-game sweep of the Padres also served as a showcase for Justice. He hit his first homer in more than three weeks, drove in four runs and pushed his batting average over .200 for the first time this season, to .208. Oh, yes, and the Braves are back to .500 at 28-28.

MONDAY, JUNE 8

This morning Justice made his professional acting debut on his favorite soap opera, "The Young and the Restless." Playing a businessman, Justice had four lines. The episode was taped and will be aired later this month. "It was fun," he said. "And yeah, I was a little nervous." He took quite a ribbing in the clubhouse later, several teammates calling him "Mr. Hollywood."

More good news on the Esasky front; he's hit another home run at Richmond. There's a feeling, however, that nothing Esasky does will get him back to Atlanta. He was a Cox signing as a free agent in November 1989, when Cox was the Braves' general manager. And Schuerholz has never seemed to warm to him. Besides, there's no real indication Esasky is over his problems with vertigo.

Today's practical joke was perpetrated in the Dodgers' dugout. Pitcher Tom Candiotti normally loves to play them, but this time he was the victim. It started when Candiotti got a call from someone claiming to be the host of a TV show called "Beautiful Homes of California" who wanted Candiotti to appear with his girlfriend, Donna Beck. What really happened, though, was that Beck set up the hoax for a Fox television show called "Payback," where practical joke victims get even in front of a hidden camera. Candiotti had just bought a new home in Bel-Air and was eager to show it off. But during the phony show that afternoon, the "host" asked Beck if she would be interested in being a co-host and traveling around the world with him. She said yes. Candiotti was speechless.

"I'm trying to be nice on this show and they're trying to steal my girlfriend," he said later. "I was ready to walk off." Only when the show's credits began to roll did he realize it was all a practical joke.

FRIDAY, JUNE 12

After a 5-1 record on the road trip, the Braves returned home for 12 games, winning the first one 6-4 over the Padres. But there was unrest in the clubhouse from Sanders and Nixon, who were tired of platooning. Sanders found it especially irritating. "It's all there in

In a 9-4 win over the Padres, David Justice hit his first homer in more than three weeks, drove in four runs and pushed his batting average over .200 for the first time this season.

JONATHAN NEWTON

black and white," he said. "Don't ever write that this is a platoon because the only time they play me is to give somebody a rest." Sanders was particularly upset that he wasn't in the lineup against righthander Andy Benes, against whom he had gone 3-for-4 last week. He sat at his locker for 20 minutes, as Glavine and Pendleton went up to him to ask if he was all right. I went to Cox. "I'm trying to be as fair about it as I can," he said. Sanders, however, was having none of it. "I keep doing the job for that guy and what happens? I'm on the bench," he said. "Damn it, any manager should know that he should find room for a guy hitting .333. Shoot, look at our other outfielders other than Nixon. They're not doing squat."

MONDAY, JUNE 15

Sometimes covering baseball has nothing to do with covering baseball. I got a call from one of my editors who told me that Nixon's girlfriend had filed for divorce. Girlfriend? Divorce? The things you

> *"Any manager should know he should find room for a guy hitting .333. Our other outfielders other than Nixon are not doing squat."*
>
> DEION SANDERS, ON HAVING TO PLATOON WITH HIS FRIEND OTIS NIXON

learn. I found out that Melissa Alfred, 26, who lived with Nixon at his house in Alpharetta, was indeed attempting to "divorce" Nixon, with whom she claimed to have a common-law marriage. She also claimed she was two months pregnant and charged that Nixon was having "continued and uncondoned adultery." Nixon said this all was news to him and immediately called Alfred at her family's home in Alabama. She told him it was true. Publicly, Nixon had nothing to say. Privately, he was furious. Alfred was claiming she and Nixon entered into a common-law marriage on April 20, 1991, and that she had helped Nixon through his drug rehabilitation. In her suit, Alfred was asking for the house, a Mercedes-Benz he gave her with the legend "O's Lady" on the front, alimony and future child support. Nixon was upset that I would have anything to do with this story, but I explained to him that the filing of the divorce suit was a matter of public record, and he was a public figure.

The next day, the suit would bring about one of the funniest incidents of the year. "You're not going to believe it," Sanders told me. "My wife comes up to me this morning with your article and points to it and says, 'What is this uncondomed adultery? Why isn't Otis using protection?'"

Eventually, Nixon had the last laugh, thanks to some good background checking by his attorneys. They discovered that on the date Alfred claimed she and Nixon entered into their common-law marriage, she was still legally married to another man. They waited until Alfred's lawyer was making a presentation in court to reveal this development. The suit was dropped. "I was planning on marrying her," said Nixon. "She could have had everything."

WEDNESDAY, JUNE 17

Blauser was in one of his Rodney Dangerfield "I get no respect" moods. We were talking about the All-Star ballot, specifically a couple of seasons ago when he got the fewest votes of anybody. This year, said Blauser, "My mother probably wrote Rafael Belliard's name on the ballot." A few days before, he had hit a two-run homer in a 4-2 win over San Diego. Interviewed by a local TV guy after the game, he deadpanned that he was trying to hit a line drive to the shortstop and get Nixon doubled off. "I was calling somebody today," he said, "and a girl gets on and says she saw where I was trying to hit into a double play. The station actually showed that."

The 4-3 win over the Dodgers finished off a three-game sweep and extended their winning streak to seven games. Next in town were the Reds, who led the Braves by 3½ games. Another sweep and first place would be Atlanta's.

A capacity crowd was on hand for the opener at Atlanta-Fulton County Stadium. Actually, it was more than capacity, for the Braves had oversold the stadium, angering hundreds of fans who found they had no seats. To compound the bad feelings, the Reds won 7-5 as Stanton gave up a 10th-inning homer to pinch hitter Glenn Braggs.

"My mother probably wrote Rafael Belliard's name on the ballot."

JEFF BLAUSER,
TALKING ABOUT
THE LACK OF RESPECT
HE RECEIVES IN
ALL-STAR VOTING

But even with their chance of overtaking the Reds in this series gone, the Braves rallied to win the next three. Cincinnati's lead was cut to a game and a half.

The Reds series was the beginning of a string of 25 straight scoreless innings by Mercker. On Friday night, he pitched 1 1/3 innings of relief for the victory in a 3-2 win. On Saturday, he earned his first save since July 1991 in a 2-1 win. And on Sunday, Bielecki and Mercker shot out the Reds 2-0. "I didn't learn anything new about myself," said Mercker. "I've always had confidence in myself. I just never have had the opportunity."

WEDNESDAY, JUNE 24

Smoltz closed out the homestand with a two-hit, 5-0 win over the Giants, the 11th victory in the 12 home games. They were now just one game behind the Reds. Schuerholz came down to the clubhouse for a round of handshaking. Things were going so good that Nixon homered, his first four-bagger in 545 at-bats as a Brave and only his fifth in 10 major-league seasons. "It was more shock than anything," said Gant. "I don't even think people in the stands thought it was out. I don't think they cheered until he got to home plate."

For the homestand, the Braves hit .294 with 12 home runs and outscored the opposition 53-29. They made just five errors, all of them in two games. In 110 innings, they allowed just 26 earned runs for an ERA of 2.13. They had four shutouts and five complete games, and the bullpen worked just 13 innings. The pitchers had a streak of 28 straight scoreless innings. Those were the kind of numbers to bolster a team's confidence going into a three-game set in Cincinnati, where they had lost three straight in their only previous trip. This time they felt they were better prepared. They were wrong.

FRIDAY, JUNE 26

Time on the road meant time to spend listening to baseball people spin yarns. One of my favorites was traveling secretary Bill Acree, who has been with the club almost 20 years. He recalled one tale from when he was a clubbie, and Donald Davidson was traveling secretary. "We were coming back from a game in New York and the bus driver got lost," he said. "Donald got so mad that he cursed him out. The bus driver then stopped the bus, got out and left, and everybody had to get cabs to get back to the city."

Treadway has returned. He's expecting to get some playing time, too, considering Lemke is hitting only .233. To make room, they designated Willard for assignment, which is just one of seemingly dozens of ways baseball tells its fringe players, "See you later, Charlie."

The Reds put a quick end to the Braves' euphoria, winning 7-4 after Braggs reached Avery for a grand slam in the first inning. The next day Cincinnati sent a clearer message, whipping the Braves 12-3 and chasing Leibrandt in the second inning. Cincinnati manager Lou Piniella made a private admission before the game that he very much

"I didn't learn anything new about myself. I've always had confidence in myself. I just never have had the opportunity."

KENT MERCKER,
AFTER EARNING A WIN
AND TWO SAVES IN THREE
GAMES AGAINST THE REDS

Photo: FRANK NIEMEIR

wanted to sweep the series. The next day he got his wish as the Reds won 6-5. Cincinnati's lead was back up to four games. Cox's patience with reporters was down to about one minute.

TUESDAY, JUNE 30

The office got the tape of Sanders's new Nike commercial today. It's supposed to air for the first time on July 14, during the All-Star Game, along with another new one by Bo Jackson. Sanders's ad, which promotes a cross-training shoe, features Sanders the football player, the baseball player, the dancer, the father, etc. It's narrated by fast-talking MTV comic Denis Leary and makes a big deal out of Sanders having two nicknames, Prime Time and Neon Deion. "I've got Deion and his 27 nicknames with me," says Leary. "You need a nickname? Maybe he'll lend you one."

Sanders has only one three-word line in the ad. After Leary says, "He's still hitting the bike, the weights, the road . . ." Sanders says, ". . . and the pool."

Meanwhile, the Braves celebrated being out of Cincinnati by beating the Giants 4-3 in San Francisco on back-to-back homers by Nixon (he's on fire) and Pendleton. I asked Nixon if he had cork in his bat. "Shoot," he said, "I used two different bats for both of the homers."

He used just one pitcher, though, Trevor Wilson, who has to be just a little embarrassed. Smoltz pitched a complete game, and now has won four of his last five starts. He's 9-5.

WEDNESDAY, JULY 1

A strange day. The Braves lost the game, 2-1, and a home run by Avery. In the third inning, Avery blasted a Bud Black pitch to deep right-center field. Second base umpire Jim Quick ruled that the ball had gone over the fence on one bounce. The fence at Candlestick Park is chain link, which sometimes makes it difficult to tell whether a ball lands in front of it or past it. Avery and Cox both felt it was a home run. Several innings later, in the TBS truck, a replay angle showed that the ball landed on the far side of the fence. After the game, several San Francisco players admitted that the ball landed over the fence, including right fielder Kevin Bass, who was closest to the ball. Said Cox, "What a joke. That took away some momentum from us. It's always something in this damn park."

A postscript: Just before Avery hit the ball, announcer Pete Van Wieren predicted Avery would hit a home run in a game this year. Broadcast partner Joe Simpson congratulated Van Wieren for being a prophet, only to quickly retract the sentiment when Quick made the call.

THURSDAY, JULY 2

An off day, a term that applies to ballplayers, not writers. My editors had decided that Sanders was the hottest thing since Menudo and wanted a big package on him. I took an overnight flight back from the coast, grabbed a few hours of sleep and came into the office, only to

Braves fans (and autograph seekers) turned out in record numbers all season.

JONATHAN NEWTON

ENCORE!

THE 1992 ATLANTA BRAVES

find I was supposed to write six — count 'em, six — stories on Sanders. Well, hey, that's what I do for a living, but there was just one teensy little problem. Sanders wasn't cooperating. He was getting plenty of exposure thanks to the Nike deal, and we weren't offering him the cover of Sports Illustrated, so he wasn't interested. None of this, of course, bothered my editors, who had secured extra space for the package and had to have something to put in it. Most of it really wasn't a problem, involving statistics, background, quotes from others about Sanders, etc. But the editors wanted a lot of up-close-and-personal stuff, and Sanders just doesn't let many people get up close and personal. Especially reporters.

To my rescue came Carolyn Chambers, the mother of Sanders's daughter. (I frankly don't know how else to describe her. I've heard Deion refer to her at various times as his "wife," although they're not married, and his "female." To me, though, she was a godsend.) She was more than happy to talk to me about their home life, about the house in Alpharetta with 11 televisions, about the pool shaped like a football and accompanying whirlpool spa shaped like a baseball, complete with stitches on the bottom, about the stable of cars that includes two Mercedes-Benzes, a truck, an Acura, a Corvette, a Chrysler LeBaron and a Lincoln Continental, about the closets with more than 100 suits and 600 pairs of shoes.

But the most interesting part of my interview with Chambers was what she told me about Deion's relationship with their 2-year-old daughter, Deiondra. "He is so protective of her," she said. "I think we have to be the only people that never bought a crib. She sleeps with us and they are so cute together. She calls him 'Da-Da' and he just loves it."

I loved that anecdote. It offered a picture of Sanders far removed from the brash, trash-talking superstar that was the only side he let most of the public see. This was a Deion anyone could relate to.

After the big package came out, Sanders and I never really talked again, save for a few words here and there. "Why do you guys have to always write about me?" he asked. "Write about someone else."

FRIDAY, JULY 3

Would the Cubs ever score again in Atlanta? That had to be the question Chicago was asking itself after Glavine beat the Cubs 3-0 for his 12th win and fifth shutout. It extended the Cubs' scoreless streak in Atlanta to 39 innings. Said first baseman Mark Grace, "I think we need to kill a chicken or something." Glavine's win gave him a 12-3 record and made him a lock to start for the NL in the All-Star Game for the second straight year.

Tom Glavine's win over the Cubs gave him a 12-3 record and made him a lock to start for the NL in the All-Star Game for the second straight year.

NICK ARROYO

JONATHAN NEWTON

The tomahawk chop was back in 1992,
among fans of all ages and all persuasions.

JONATHAN NEWTON

The next day, the Cubs broke their scoreless string at 46 2/3 innings when they touched Leibrandt for two runs in the eighth. But the Braves won 4-2 to remain three back of the Reds.

While the Braves were beating the Cubs, Schuerholz was coming back from Brazil, where he'd gone on a scouting trip with director of scouting Chuck LaMar and special assistant Paul Snyder. They went to South America to try to sign a 6-foot-6, 16-year-old right-handed pitcher named Jose Pett. If he lived in the U.S., Pett would have been the first high school player taken in the amateur draft. Unfortunately for Schuerholz and Co., he ended up signing with Toronto.

SUNDAY, JULY 5

Another shutout, but this time it was the Cubs on top, 8-0 behind Greg Maddux. The big story, however, was a fan being ejected from the game for giving home-plate umpire Bill Hohn the finger. The incident took place in the fourth inning after Hohn called Pendleton out on strikes. Pendleton went in the dugout and yelled something at Hohn, who came over and threatened to throw him out. Cox came out and was ejected. Then Hohn, his temper not helped by the 90-degree heat, noticed a fan behind the home-plate screen making a hand gesture. He asked a security guard to throw him out. I went running down to the gate where the fan was being taken out and asked him his name. He would only identify himself as Billy from Bremen. "Maybe I deserved it," he said. "But I was angry at the call. And it's a free country." Instead of being thrown out of the park, though, "Billy" was merely escorted to another seat. After the game, I talked to umpire crew chief John McSherry. He said he would speak to Hohn, who was standing only a few feet away, smiling. McSherry admitted it was an unusual thing to do, but backed up Hohn's call. "Bill wanted to stop it right there and made the call," he said. Added Hohn, "It was too damn hot out there to put up with crap like that."

MONDAY, JULY 6

A 3-1 loss to the Mets was overshadowed by a major development in the commissioner's office. Commissioner Fay Vincent ordered the National League to realign for the 1993 season, when the Florida Marlins will join the East Division and the Colorado Rockies the West. Citing the commissioner's power to act "in the best interests of baseball," Vincent ordered the Chicago Cubs and St. Louis Cardinals to shift from the East to the West, and the Braves and Cincinnati Reds from the West to the East. The move makes geographic sense, since both St. Louis and Chicago are west of Atlanta and Cincinnati, but Vincent's decision caused some problems.

The NL clubs had voted 10-2 in favor of realignment, but one of the negative votes was cast by the Cubs, who don't want to play in the West because it would mean more West Coast games and late starting times. They say the smaller audiences for late-night starts would hurt their advertising sales on WGN, which broadcasts their games. Just as

Umpire Bill Hohn, his temper not helped by the 90-degree heat, noticed a fan behind the home-plate screen making a hand gesture. He asked a security guard to throw him out.

RICH MAHAN

the Braves and the cable channel that carries their games, WTBS, are owned by the same people, so are the Cubs and their broadcaster, WGN.

A provision in the NL constitution gives a team that would be affected by realignment the right to veto it, so the Cubs' vote should have killed it. That's where Vincent stepped in and overrode the veto, which angered a lot of owners. It wasn't so much that they were opposed to realignment; they merely felt Vincent had no right to act unilaterally. The Braves are torn on this issue. They've been trying to get out of the NL West for years, but they're leery of supporting Vincent because they know he's opposed to the influence superstations such as WGN and WTBS wield in baseball.

The night's other story was Bobby Bonilla, the outfielder the Mets signed away from the Pittsburgh Pirates for close to $6 million a year. He's been having a tough time in New York, and the papers have been killing him. In the fourth inning, plate umpire Harry Wendelstedt

"Shoot, the media is pussycats down here compared to them. They'll rip your wife, your family, your dog."

GREG OLSON, ON BOBBY BONILLA'S PLIGHT WITH THE NEW YORK MEDIA

threw him out for arguing a strike-two call. Afterward, Wendelstedt said Bonilla told him, "You can't look at me." "I didn't realize his holiness had risen to that rank," Wendlestedt said. "Bobby has always been a gentleman. I like Bobby as a person. But the pressure cooker has gotten to him."

It gets to a lot of them. I asked Olson if he could imagine how some of the Braves who felt the Atlanta press was too tough on them would fare in New York. "Shoot," he said, "the media is pussycats down here compared to them. They'll rip your wife, your family, your dog."

These New York writers are quite a group. Despite being competitors, they stick together, and they aren't intimidated by anyone. Said Bob Klapisch of the *New York Daily News*, "[Mets manager] Jeff Torborg tried to come in here and be tough and show us something. That didn't last long. He learned his lesson very quickly. Bobby Bonilla hasn't." Whew. Remind me never to irritate these guys.

ENCORE!

LOUIE FAVORITE

WEDNESDAY, JULY 8

For the first time in six years, the Braves have a non-pitching starter on the All-Star team. Pendleton was elected by the fans at third base, edging San Diego's Gary Sheffield by 67,000 votes. The last Brave to be chosen a starter in the field was outfielder Dale Murphy in 1986. Pendleton was almost apologetic about beating out Sheffield, who is having a heck of a season. "It's nothing against the fans, and I really appreciate them voting for me," he said, "but Gary has better numbers."

He was right: Sheffield led Pendleton in average, .316 to .303; home runs, 17 to 13; and runs batted in, 58 to 51. Still, you had to feel good for Pendleton, who got jobbed last year when he didn't even make the team as a reserve despite a .324 average. Sheffield at least is a lock to be named as a reserve. Cox, who'll manage the NL team and thus gets to name pitchers and reserves, privately told me that both Gant and Smoltz would make the team too. And Glavine will be the

All-Star starter Terry Pendleton was almost apologetic about beating out Gary Sheffield, who was having a heck of a season

starter for the second straight year.

The next day, when Cox made his reserve picks, the Reds were upset. Cox picked Cincinnati reliever Norm Charlton and second baseman Bip Roberts, but several Reds thought that at least one more should have been selected from among pitchers Greg Swindell, Tim Belcher and Scott Bankhead, and shortstop Barry Larkin. Swindell was so mad when he found out, he threw a half-full soft drink container at the wall and stalked into the trainer's room.

Cox was hardly sympathetic. The year before, Piniella had bypassed Pendleton and Gant in favor of two of his own players, third baseman Chris Sabo and outfielder Paul O'Neill. Cox hadn't forgotten. This, he said privately, was a little payback.

SUNDAY, JULY 12

Nothing like a little four-game sweep to put you in a good mood going into the All-Star break. Not to mention cut the Reds' lead to two games. In the first game at Chicago's Wrigley Field, Lemke tripled home two runs in the 12th for a 2-0 win. The next night, Smoltz won 4-0, the Braves' sixth shutout of the Cubs in 10 games. The Cubs would have enjoyed seeing what happened to the Braves later that night at their hotel. There was some sort of high school convention at the Hyatt Regency, and the little darlings had taken over the elevators, punching the buttons for every floor of the 30-story building. Most of the Braves' party gave up on getting an elevator and used the stairs instead. Bream, who had spent much of the game in the training room because of a stomach virus, walked up 25 flights. Susan Bielecki, six months pregnant, walked up 14 floors. She was not amused.

On Friday night, Sanders who was in an 0-for-12 slump, asked Blauser to take the hex off him. Blauser's "cure" was kissing Sanders. I'm not sure it was worth it, but it worked, for Sanders won the Saturday night game with an eighth-inning home run.

Before the game, Nixon showed me the array of electronic gadgets he brings with him on the road. He had one machine that could transmit faxes, and contained an electronic dictionary, "so I can understand all those big words Blauser throws at me," he said. He also had a cellular phone, a laptop computer where he kept his files on pitchers' pickoff moves, a video Walkman with 40 eight-millimeter tapes (some of which you definitely had to be over 18 to watch), an electronic encyclopedia, relaxation glasses, a laser pen, a skypager and a camera and tape recorder that fit inside a pen. No wonder he plans on opening his own electronics store.

In the finale, Blauser hit three homers in a 7-4 win that wrapped up Atlanta's first four-game sweep of the Cubs since 1967. Peña got his fourth save in the last five games.

Now the club split up, with a big contingent going to the All-Star game and the rest going home. They had three days to rest up for the second half of the season.

Mark Lemke tripled home two runs in the 12th inning for a 2-0 win over the Cubs, starting a four-game winning streak going into the All-Star break.

WALTER STRICKLIN

ENCORE!

Terry Pendleton was the only Brave to have any success at all in the All-Star Game, getting a single off Boston's Roger Clemens.

DAVID TULIS

ENCORE!

THURSDAY, JULY 16

The All-Star Game in San Diego will not go down as one of the season's sweetest memories for the Braves who were involved. Glavine got shelled, giving up a record seven straight singles and a total of five runs in 1 2/3 innings. Gant grounded out and popped up. Smoltz allowed a single to the only batter he faced. Only Pendleton salvaged any small measure of glory, getting a single off Boston fireballer Roger Clemens in two at-bats. And Cox managed the National League to its fifth straight loss, a 13-6 decision.

Cox should have known it wouldn't be an Atlanta night. The previous evening at the big All-Star gala, his daughter Skyla had encountered a robot who could do the tomahawk chop. But when Cox asked it who would win the NL West, it had told him the Padres would. After all, it was a San Diego robot.

There was plenty of reason for optimism, however, as the second half of the season started in Houston. A year before, the Braves had come out of the break 9 1/2 games behind the Dodgers. This time they trailed the Reds by two. And they immediately cut that in half with a 4-2 win over the Astros while the Reds were losing to the Cardinals.

FRIDAY, JULY 17

Esasky is done. This was the date on which the Braves had agreed either to bring him up from Richmond or release him. They wanted him to spend more time in the minors. He wasn't willing to do that, so they released him. They would have to eat his $1.95 million salary.

For the $5.6 million they paid him over three years, this was the total return on the Braves' investment: nine games, 35 at-bats, six hits (a .171 average), two runs, no homers, no RBIs, no extra-base hits, four walks and 14 strikeouts. No one was saying it was his fault, for surely he had no control over the mysterious vertigo that overtook him. You couldn't help but feel sorry for the guy. The Braves, though they had to pay him the full value of the contract, had done him a favor by letting him play in the minors so he could showcase whatever ability he managed to recover. They felt that the least he could do in return was to play out the contract, just in case an emergency should arise and they might need him.

Needless to say, he didn't see it that way. The night he was released, I must have called his house a hundred times. Sometimes his daughter answered, other times the message machine did. I didn't reach him until the next day. "I don't feel that criticism is warranted," he said. "I felt I did everything I could do. I can look into the mirror at myself and say that I went through a number of tests, through rehabilitation, to extended spring training and back and forth to Richmond. I feel I'm ready to play in the major leagues and the Braves didn't have room."

As it turned out, no one else agreed with him. He didn't sign with anyone else the rest of the season.

Before the game, in which Smoltz would shut out the Astros 5-0,

For the $5.6 million they paid Nick Esasky over three years, this was the total return on the Braves' investment: nine games, 35 at-bats, six hits, no homers, no RBIs.

WALTER STRICKLIN

I sat with Mazzone listening to his tales from the minor leagues. This is a guy who once was kicked out of the Mexican League when his team owner tried to pass him off as Mexican. Another time, he said, "I was in the Midwest League in Decatur, Illinois, in 1969 when a few of my teammates decided to pull a prank on me and forge a draft notice, complete with a presidential seal. The manager was in on the gag, and they gave it to me during the game. When I finally found out it was a phony, I ran after my buddy and the manager tackled me. Everybody was laughing, including the other team, which had been told what was going on."

John Smoltz's 5-0 shutout of the Astros gave the Braves six straight wins and cut the Reds' lead to one game.

SUNDAY, JULY 19

The winning streak reached nine games with a 3-2, 10-inning victory over the Astros that completed a four-game sweep in Houston.

They remained one game behind the Reds, who rallied from a four-run deficit to knock off the Cardinals 5-4. The Braves had now won all six games they had played at the Astrodome, perhaps the toughest place for visiting teams to play in over the last 20 years. Going back to 1991, the Braves had won 13 of 15 there. In the 37 innings of this four-game series, the Astros scored just four runs, and struck out more times (27) than they got hits (25).

The big rumor of the day was the Braves seriously considering trading for Seattle second baseman Harold Reynolds. Seattle's George Zuraw, the assistant to general manager Woody Woodward, was in town asking about Mercker, Wohlers and minor-league pitcher David Nied. Schuerholz was looking for an everyday second baseman, not convinced that either Lemke or Treadway was the long-term answer. Nothing ever came of it, though.

FRANK NIEMEIR

The Braves traded unhappy reliever Juan Berenguer to Kansas City for free-agent bust Mark Davis.

TUESDAY, JULY 21

Big news in St. Louis. The Braves traded Berenguer to Kansas City for reliever Mark Davis. Giving up Berenguer wasn't that surprising — he wasn't happy, Peña had taken over the closer's role, and Wohlers or Mercker could fill in if Peña faltered — but getting Davis? The guy was one of the biggest busts in the history of free agency. He'd won the NL Cy Young Award after saving 44 games for the Padres in 1989, after which he signed as a free agent with the Royals for $12.8 million over four years. His two full seasons with the Royals, he was a combined 8-10 with a 4.80 ERA. This year he was 1-3, 7.18. No, this deal made no sense, until you recalled who signed Davis for the big bucks in Kansas City — Schuerholz. Davis was a messy splotch of road kill on Schuerholz's otherwise spotless reputation, but it would be the dry cleaning job of the century if the left-hander could resurrect himself with the Braves. Schuerholz would look like a genius. Schuerholz liked looking like a genius.

Tommy Gregg didn't think Schuerholz was a genius, though. I couldn't print what Gregg thought of him after Schuerholz, without giving him any notice, optioned him to Richmond. He was already there on an injury-rehab assignment, but this meant he wasn't coming back to Atlanta. "At least they could have had the courtesy to give me a call and tell me," said Gregg, fuming. Instead, Richmond manager Chris Chambliss had to give him the news.

WEDNESDAY, JULY 22

First place! Behind another strong performance by Smoltz, the Braves won their 11th straight game, a 2-0 shutout of the Cardinals. They now led the Reds by a half-game. The streak was the longest in baseball this season and just two wins shy of the franchise record, set in 1982 when the Braves won their first 13 games.

Davis arrived, and all the writers wanted to talk about his troubles. He was reluctant at first, but gradually opened up. If he thought leaving K.C. meant putting his past behind him, he was wrong.

We were back home, and the Pirates were in town. The streak reached 12 as Glavine won his 15th game — tops in the majors — by beating Pittsburgh 4-3. Yet even with his record 15-3, rumors have begun that Glavine may have lost five miles per hour off his fastball and may be hurt. One who has been espousing this theory is ESPN's Gammons. "I heard that the other day in St. Louis," said Glavine. "I don't know where he got that from. I don't feel like I've lost anything. But if I did, I don't know if it would matter because I'm still getting people out."

W.A. BRIDGES JR.

SATURDAY, JULY 25

What a night. The franchise-record winning streak was equaled, and Nixon made the play of the year. Of his life. The Braves were up 1-0 in the ninth inning, but the Pirates had a runner on and Andy Van Slyke at the plate facing Peña with one out. Van Slyke drove the ball deep to center field. Watching in the bullpen, Mercker said to himself, "It's gone." At the crack of the bat, Nixon turned and sprinted toward the fence. When he got there, he leaped as high as he could, stretching his gloved left hand over the top of the 10-foot-high fence. It was enough, barely. The ball snagged in his glove, which he yanked back so it wouldn't be knocked off his hand by the top of the fence. When Bonds grounded to first a few moments later, the Braves had their 13th consecutive win.

"It's just a reaction play," said Nixon. "I thought it was going to be out, but that I might have a chance. I don't remember a lot about it. It's not something you go out and practice during batting practice."

Before the final out was made, "The Catch" was replayed several times on the giant video screen above the center-field stands. Even the players watched. When the game was over, instead of mobbing the pitcher, the Braves reserves rushed to greet Nixon.

"It gave me the chills," he said. "Even when I got the stolen-base record, it was nothing like this."

Was there another miracle left to produce a 14th straight win? Almost. The Pirates blew a three-run lead the next night, but scored a run in the ninth to win 5-4. The streak had allowed the Braves to make up seven games on the Reds, and now Atlanta led by one.

"It gave me the chills. Even when I got the stolen-base record, it was nothing like this."

OTIS NIXON, ON THE REACTION TO "THE CATCH," HIS LEAPING GRAB THAT SAVED A 1-0 VICTORY AND GAVE THE BRAVES A RECORD-TYING 13TH STRAIGHT WIN

TUESDAY, JULY 28

Nixon's drug awareness film, "Strikeout," was about to be released. Nixon put up $175,000 to have it made, and it was to be distributed through school systems around the state. Nixon let me watch it on his hand-held VCR. The movie takes the viewer through the baseball career of fictional character Chris Jones, who is played by actor Morris Chesnut, who starred in "Boyz in the Hood." It opens with a group of young black men being shot at, and one appearing to fall right into the camera with a gunshot wound in his head. In the final scene, Jones is depicted in a back alley, his career at a low point,

Photo: W.A. BRIDGES JR.

shooting a drug into his arm. There will be a longer version of the film, which will end with Jones dying. The story is narrated by several athletes, including heavyweight champion Evander Holyfield, wrestler Zeus, and Braves Lonnie Smith, Blauser, Sanders, Justice and Glavine. Justice is the most convincing actor among the athletes.

The Braves, meanwhile, were having problems with their bullpen, blowing a lead against the Astros for the second straight night. But there was worse news. The club's streak of 258 games without a pitcher missing a start because of an injury was over. Bielecki heard a pop in his elbow. He was headed for surgery. Pete Smith would be headed back to Atlanta.

WEDNESDAY, JULY 29

Public relations assistant Glen Serra pulled a great joke on Olson. He told the catcher that Miss Georgia had asked to meet him, so Olson put on his game uniform and went to the bathroom mirror to check his hair (what there is of it). Serra then escorted Olson to a room outside the clubhouse, and there she was. Not Miss Georgia, but Little Miss Georgia, 8-year-old Heather Miranda Vargas. Olson knew he'd been had, but he took it all in good humor.

Score one for Avery over Sanders in the joke department. Avery twice tried — unsuccessfully — to set Sanders's shoelaces on fire. Looking for revenge, Sanders crawled behind Avery and set *his* shoelaces on fire. What he didn't realize was that Avery had put on a pair of Sanders's shoes. So Avery let the laces burn all the way down.

FRIDAY, JULY 31

This originally was to be Sanders's final day with the Braves before leaving to join the Falcons, but he decided to stay with the baseball team indefinitely. He couldn't come to an agreement with the Braves on a long-term deal — he wanted $3 million a year — but decided to stay on with an extension of his contract. "There's no reason to leave now," he said. The Braves had been getting along all right even without Sanders in the lineup. Nixon was doing the job at the leadoff spot, and Sanders had been bothered with various nagging injuries.

With the Braves in San Francisco, Sanders and Nixon took time to visit the new $12 million house of rapper Hammer in nearby San Jose. Getting there was no problem; Hammer sent his limo. Upon their return, they described the place in glowing terms, recalling a bedroom of 50 feet by 50 feet, a transparent fireplace, a $300,000 stereo system, an indoor pool and an 11-car garage. Oh, yes, and a solid-gold toilet seat. Sanders didn't want me to write about that, because the house wasn't finished and he was concerned someone might steal the seat. OK, I covered up the toilet seat story. So sue me.

Apparently the surroundings didn't sufficiently inspire the Braves, for they lost the game that night 4-3. Mercker watched his 25 2/3-innings scoreless streak come to an end, and the Braves watched the Reds pass them by a half-game.

Deion Sanders was once again the center of attention when he decided to stay with the Braves rather than join the Falcons on Aug. 1.

Previous page: JONATHAN NEWTON

CHAPTER 6

JOURNEY TO THE TOP

SUNDAY, AUG. 2

A RARE DOUBLEHEADER LOOKED LIKE IT WAS GOING TO catch the Braves with their pitching down. Pete Smith was scheduled to pitch the opener, but Glavine told Cox he didn't feel comfortable pitching on three days' rest, so they brought up Armando Reynoso from Richmond to pitch the second game. With a No. 5 starter (and a replacement one at that) and a minor-league callup pitching, it appeared there was a good chance the Braves could be swept. But they were the ones who did the sweeping, beating the Giants 3-0 and 8-5.

"I'll take the end result and get the hell out of here before they realize what happened," said a relieved Pendleton.

In the second game, Olson had to catch Reynoso for the first time, not an easy task considering he doesn't speak Spanish and Reynoso doesn't speak English. When Reynoso pitched for the Braves in '91, Cabrera caught him. Said Olson, "I called Frankie last night for some advice." Reynoso allowed four runs in five innings, and left trailing 4-2, but got credit for the win when the Braves scored six runs in the top of the sixth. He was sent back to Richmond the next day.

With a No. 5 starter and a minor-league callup pitching, there was a good chance the Braves could be swept. But they were the ones who did the sweeping, beating the Giants 3-0 and 8-5.

WILLIAM BERRY

Pete Smith, making his first start of the season, shut out the Giants in the first game of a doubleheader.

ENCORE!

MONDAY, AUG. 3

Armageddon loomed. The Reds were coming to Atlanta for what would be the biggest series of the season to date. Atlanta-Fulton County Stadium had been sold out for months for these three games.

The Braves hoped that the home-field advantage would continue to play a major role in the series. The Reds had won all six games in Cincinnati; the Braves, three of four in Atlanta. Cincinnati manager Piniella was optimistic, primarily because his club was healthier than it had been in some time. Third baseman Sabo was back in the lineup, and outfielder Reggie Sanders had come off the disabled list. "I think we'll go to Atlanta nice and relaxed," Piniella said.

I had been keeping in touch with *Cincinnati Post* beat writer Jerry Crasnick, who told me the Reds felt they could win at least two of the three games, retake first place, go back home to Cincinnati and start to gain some distance on the Braves. It was far too early in the season for this series to be crucial, but it could play a large role in giving the winner confidence.

Both clubs were confident going in, but the Braves had an added advantage. The day off enabled them to juggle their rotation, moving Smoltz ahead of Leibrandt into the third-game starting role, behind Glavine and Avery. The three Young Guns were ready to fire.

TUESDAY, AUG. 4

Baseball's publicity people came up with an interesting statistic today, although for the life of me I don't know how they figured it out. They claimed that Blauser's home run on July 4 was the 1,776th major-league homer hit on Independence Day. Blauser was impressed. "I did it for my country," he said.

On a slightly more serious note, I went over to Sanders's locker to talk to him about his latest meeting with the Falcons' management. Word was these talks weren't going well, but I wanted to hear for myself. Unfortunately, a TV cameraman had annoyed Sanders by being a little too persistent, and Sanders retreated to the training room. A few minutes later, Belliard emerged from the training room with a piece of paper that he taped above Sanders's locker. It read this way:

The Reds felt they could win at least two of the three games, retake first place, go back home to Cincinnati and start to gain some distance on the Braves.

1. No.
2. Yes.
3. No.
4. No.
5. No.
6. Yes.
7. Thank you.
8. Maybe.
9. It will be up to my daughter.
(signed) Deion

That night's game changed the course of the season. It appeared that Glavine's 10-game winning streak was over, with the Reds leading 5-2 in the eighth and Norm Charlton on the mound. He already had 24 saves, including two against Atlanta, but gave up three runs in the eighth as the Braves tied it 5-5. In the ninth Charlton got the first two outs, but walked Nixon, who then stole second. Pendleton, who had nine hits in his 12 previous at-bats with runners in scoring position, was surprised he wasn't walked with a base open. "I'm not trying to be arrogant or cocky," he said. "I personally wouldn't have wanted to pitch to me." Charlton threw his trademark pitch, a forkball, and Pendleton hammered it off the "Hank Aaron 715" sign beyond the left-field fence for a two-run homer. Afterward, Piniella was asked why he had Charlton pitch to Pendleton. He responded with silence.

JONATHAN NEWTON

Tension was thick as the Reds came to town trailing by half a game. Behind solid pitching by Steve Avery and John Smoltz, the Braves won three straight to pad their lead.

WEDNESDAY, AUG. 5

Another Cincinnati loss, but more important for the Reds was the players they lost to injury. First baseman Hal Morris pulled a hamstring in the on-deck circle and would miss the next four weeks. Then center fielder Bip Roberts went head-first into the wall chasing a ball hit by Justice. For 15 minutes, the crowd hushed as trainers attended to Roberts, who was flat on his back. They placed his neck in a brace and he was put on a cart and sent off to Piedmont Hospital. A CAT scan and X-rays on his neck and spine were negative, but he was out indefinitely. The Braves won 5-1 on back-to-back homers by Bream and Berryhill as Avery picked up his ninth win.

THURSDAY, AUG. 6

For Smoltz, this was a chance to finish the Braves' first three-game sweep of the Reds since 1982. He said he would approach the game "like it was one in the playoffs," and that was bad news for Cincinnati, because Smoltz had been the Braves most consistent pitcher in the 1991 postseason. Once again he came through, going the distance

Photo: JONATHAN NEWTON

Damon Berryhill missed the tag,
but Brett Butler missed the plate
as the Braves took two of three
from the Dodgers.

WILLIAM BERRY

ENCORE!

in a 5-3 win that left the Braves 3 1/2 games up on the Reds, Atlanta's biggest division lead all season. Piniella had come into the series saying that "as long as nobody got swept, the race would go on." Now, it was tough even to get him to say the obligatory "There's still a lot of baseball left." But the Braves weren't ready to claim anything yet. Said Olson, "There isn't one guy here that is going home and jumping up and down in the bedroom because they think this race is over."

SUNDAY, AUG. 9

In a feature story on Smoltz, *Journal-Constitution* reporter Jeff Schultz noted that the pitcher played the accordion as a kid. Smoltz got a nice ribbing from his teammates, but I discovered that some other players were musically inclined when they were young. Bream, for instance, said he played the trumpet until the eighth grade. But the best story came from dugout coach Jim Beauchamp, who played trumpet in high school. "We were once in Montreal and I was coming out of the tunnel into the dugout," he said. "There was this band that was about to go on the field and I grabbed the trumpet and played 'Oh Susannah.'"

Streaking. Sunday's 10-3 win over the Dodgers was the ninth straight victory for the team, the 11th in a row for Glavine, who became baseball's first 17-game winner of '92. The streak ended the next day, but not without an accompanying bizarre incident. In the bottom of the fifth inning, with Nixon at the plate, the sprinklers came on. "I thought someone had thrown a bucket of water," said a startled Nixon. Because the Braves had played a day game the day before, the sprinklers had been set to come on automatically at 9 p.m. No one remembered to change the timer to accommodate a night game. The Dodgers won 5-3, but the crowd of 43,368 gave the Braves an Atlanta single-season attendance record of 2,156,715.

THURSDAY, AUG. 13

The Padres were in town, and I was talking to visitors clubhouse manager John Holland and assistant Fred Stone about the special requests he gets. Tony Gwynn wants him to hook Gwynn's portable VCR up to the television in Holland's office. Lasorda wants cut-up watermelon and cantaloupe. Philadelphia's Kruk asks him to send out for Kentucky Fried Chicken. For Pittsburgh's Bonds, it's Pizza Hut pizza.

The Padres had started to insinuate themselves into the race. When they beat the Braves in the opener of their series Tuesday, they trailed Atlanta by 5 1/2 games, Cincinnati by four. Through eight innings on Thursday, the Padres and Braves were tied 3-3. But with one out in the ninth, pinch hitter Berryhill homered off Larry Andersen for a 4-3 win.

I wanted to say, "I told you so." Before the bottom of the ninth began, I had turned to *San Diego Tribune* writer Barry Bloom and said, "This one is over." "No way, no way. Want to bet?" he asked.

"Ten bucks," I said. (Memo to the IRS: I never collected.)

The win ended the homestand at 7-2. Ahead was another big test — trips to Pittsburgh and Montreal, whose Pirates and Expos were battling for the East title.

FRIDAY, AUG. 14

Massacre at Three Rivers Stadium. The Braves pounded the Pirates 15-0, achieving season highs in hits (22) and runs. The Atlanta linescore for the first three innings looked like one of Smoltz's golf scorecards — 4-4-3. Lonnie Smith had career-high numbers in hits (5) and RBIs (6), including a second-inning grand slam. Nixon and Hunter both went 4-for-6. Glavine coasted to go 18-3. For the Pirates, it was their most lopsided loss in 16 years.

Smith was more cordial than usual after the game. It didn't necessarily have anything to do with his performance, either. He wasn't one of these guys who talked only when he was going good. No, Smith was just as likely to be surly after a 4-for-4 night as an 0-for-4. But his impending free agency after the season seemed to have mellowed him somewhat. And he was playing a little more, as Cox was giving Gant and Justice some days off.

SUNDAY, AUG. 16

The Pirates finally discovered the Braves' weakness: They're clueless against a knuckleball pitcher. For eight innings, they flailed away fruitlessly against rookie Tim Wakefield, a converted infielder. Olson knocked in two runs with a double in the ninth, but that wasn't enough to overcome a 4-0 deficit. If the Pirates and Braves were to meet again in the playoffs, Wakefield could prove to be a big factor.

WEDNESDAY, AUG. 19

Glavine's 13th straight win tied a franchise record that dated back to 1884, and gave the Braves a 6 1/2-game lead over the Reds. But all was not right. Nixon was upset about not playing, especially because the game was in Montreal, where he had played three years for the Expos. He had left 15 tickets for friends, and he was embarrassed. He didn't leave the clubhouse for the dugout until the fifth inning.

Nixon felt he should be in the lineup every day, but he didn't think Sanders was the problem. He felt they both should play, with either Justice or Gant sitting out on a game-by-game basis. Justice and Gant had only two home runs between them in the last month, but Nixon never really pushed Cox hard on the issue.

Before the road trip ended Thursday, bullpen coach Ned Yost had managed to take a trip to the top of Olympic Stadium, to the stuck-open retractable roof some 185 feet above the playing surface. "One of the guys working on the roof asked if I could give them a baseball," Yost explained. "I said, 'Yeah, if you can take me to the top of the roof.' I thought he was just kidding, but he said to show up the next day at 2. I did, and sure enough he was there."

The Pirates finally discovered the Braves' weakness: They're clueless against a knuckleball pitcher.

112

WILLIAM BERRY

FRIDAY, AUG. 21

Sanders was fed up with the Falcons. They hadn't moved far enough or fast enough on contract negotiations to suit him, so he decided to take the offensive in the media. Before batting practice, he called the *Journal-Constitution's* Falcons beat reporter, Len Pasquarelli, from the clubhouse on his cellular phone. He accused Falcons management of having a "plantation type of [mentality]" in its dealings with him. "This goes way back," he said, "and it's way beyond money. It goes way back to when I brought my friend Walter Sutton over there and they ran him away. . . . Well, they know where I am, right down the damned street playing baseball for the Braves, and I'm still getting fined all the time."

On Sanders's recommendation, the Falcons had drafted Sutton, who had been Sanders's childhood friend in Fort Myers, Fla. Unfortunately, after the draft, it came out that Sutton might not be able to join the Falcons right away because of this teensy little problem of a drug-selling conviction and pending sentencing. Sanders's loyalty to his friend was admirable, but he let it blind him to the obvious conclusion that the Falcons simply couldn't keep a convicted drug dealer on the roster.

Sanders's attitude toward the Falcons' negotiating stance was puzzling, too. He wasn't unsigned; he had a contract with them that he

Lonnie Smith had career-high numbers in hits (5) and RBIs (6), including a second-inning grand slam, as the Braves rocked the Pirates 15-0.

was in violation of by staying with the Braves and not reporting to training camp on time. He felt they were sticking it to him, when in fact they had kowtowed to him by offering him a $1 million bonus just to report on time. One million dollars just to honor his contract. Unbelievable.

Yet Sanders knew he could get away with virtually anything by playing one team off against the other. The Falcons were especially vulnerable because they needed him more. He was probably the best cornerback in football, and their secondary already had been weakened when Brian Jordan gave up football to join the Cardinals. Had they been a bad team, they would have been able to let Sanders go — Hey, Deion, we can lose just as easily without you as with you — but they had made the playoffs last fall; they had a brand-new stadium, the Georgia Dome; and they could smell the Super Bowl. But they couldn't get there without Sanders.

When Sanders's interview with Pasquarelli was printed in the next morning's paper, Deion apparently didn't like the way it sounded. He claimed he'd been misquoted (which was a lie; Pasquarelli had the whole thing on tape). And he made one more decision. He wasn't going to talk to anyone in the Atlanta media again.

The Braves weren't concerned about Sanders. After all, he was playing for them; let the Falcons worry about getting him back. For $6,000 a game, he would stay with the Braves for the rest of the season.

The team was much more concerned about Peña, who seemed to have lost a lot of zip off his fastball. They had his right elbow examined, but couldn't find anything wrong. That wasn't good news. At least when you find something wong, you can try to fix it. Quietly, Schuerholz began looking for bullpen help.

The Braves went seven games up on the Reds the next night with a 3-2 win over the Cardinals, Justice providing the winning hit with a two-run homer. Pete Smith pitched a complete game, hiking his record to 3-0.

Smith seemed to have changed. For a couple of years he had a reputation as the biggest womanizer on the team, with a different girl in every city. Now he claimed that had been blown out of proportion. "I didn't have a steady girlfriend, so sometimes people would see me with a new girl every week," he said.

After Smith failed to make the team in spring training, he started working on his attitude with Llewellyn. Later, as Smith experienced more success, his old cockiness would come creeping back.

TUESDAY, AUG. 25

A day of mourning, at least for Glavine and Mazzone. Larry Bird announced his retirement from the Boston Celtics, and both Glavine, who grew up near Boston, and Mazzone, a huge Celtics fan, etched Bird's No. 33 under the bill of their caps.

A bad night all around for Glavine. He was going for his 14th

On August 25, Tom Glavine lost for the first time in 95 days. During the game, he walked consecutive batters for the first time all season.

Photo: DAVID TULIS

JONATHAN NEWTON

straight win, which would have made him the first pitcher in the majors to reach 20 this season, but the Expos beat him 6-0. It was the Braves' sixth loss to Montreal in 10 games this year, and Glavine's 11th loss to the Canadian team in 14 lifetime decisions.

Glavine hadn't lost in 95 days, since back on May 22, when a 7-1 loss to — who else? — the Expos had dropped the Braves to 19-24, fourth place, and 61/2 games behind first-place San Francisco. So no one thought anything of it that for the first time this season, Glavine walked consecutive batters. Or that he walked in a run for the first time. Or that his 42/3 innings represented his shortest outing since May 17.

But there was something wrong, and only Cox, Mazzone, Schuerholz and the training staff knew about it. Glavine had sustained a hairline fracture of one of his ribs the previous week while warming up in Montreal. He could still pitch — he won his 19th game after it happened — but the pain was worsening.

The next night the Expos continued their mastery over the Braves, winning 5-4. Cincinnati won again, cutting Atlanta's lead to 31/2 games. Maybe there would be a race after all. Peña, however, wouldn't be involved in it for a couple of weeks. He was put on the 15-day disabled list with a diagnosis of tendinitis in his right elbow.

The Aug. 27 game was rained out, but not without some controversy. The Braves waited three hours and 28 minutes to make the decision, which infuriated Montreal manager Felipe Alou.

FRANK NIEMEIR

THURSDAY, AUG. 27

Sanders has made his decision. He rejected an offer from the Falcons that would have allowed him to take two weeks off during October for the playoffs and World Series. Schuerholz was ecstatic. He had kept Sanders without paying him one more cent.

The game was rained out, but not without some controversy. The Braves waited three hours and 28 minutes to make the decision, which infuriated Montreal manager Felipe Alou. "The people here were playing games with the fans and the teams," he said. "These people don't know about hurricanes, I guess. They don't know about tropical depressions or whatever. This was Hurricane Andrew, in case they didn't know, not some shower." Alou's comments angered Schuerholz, who said the forecast he had been given showed a break in the showers. (He would later send a letter to Alou saying he didn't appreciate the manager's comments. Alou would just laugh.)

FRIDAY, AUG. 28

More rain, this time in Philadelphia. For the first time all season, the Braves had lost four in a row. They blew a 3-0 lead in the top of the first by allowing the Phils to tie it in the bottom half of the inning. The final score was 7-3. Sanders did an interview with TBS, which irritated some of the Atlanta writers, with whom he no longer is speaking. Actually, it's kind of funny how this whole thing has unfolded. Terry Moore had written a column advising Sanders to stop talking. Sanders was now claiming that as the reason he has clammed up. But Sanders loathes Moore, and the idea of him doing something because Terry told him to do it is laughable. Of course, l keep forgetting that Deion did not major in logic at Florida State.

Strength and conditioning coach Frank Fultz is traveling with the club. He's been driving everybody crazy by constantly asking directions. In the clubhouse at Veterans Stadium, he was playing a game with one of the clubbies, demonstrating his mastery of a tongue twister. In 10 seconds, he could say, "One hen, two ducks, three squawking geese, four limerick oysters, five corpulent porpoises, six pair of Donovera tweezers, seven thousand Macedonians in full battle array, eight brass monkeys from the ancient sacred crypts of Egypt, nine apathetic, sympathetic, diabetic old men on roller skates and ten 10-pound cases of Mother Fletcher's Cheese." What a mouthful.

Someone else with a mouthful to say was Gant, who had hit only one home run since June 16. With only 11 homers and little more than a month left in the season, he had no shot at a third straight season with 30 homers and 30 stolen bases. Perhaps it was frustration that led him to say fans in Atlanta "are stupid. They boo you instead of being behind you. They say things to me in the outfield. But one of the good things about this team is we don't worry about what they say and what is written."

Sure you don't, Ron. And I'll probably be running into the Pope down at the synagogue, too.

JONATHAN NEWTON

"They boo you instead of being behind you. They say things to me in the outfield. But one of the good things about this team is we don't worry about what they say."

RON GANT,
ON FAN REACTION TO HIS
SECOND-HALF STRUGGLES

ENCORE!

CHAPTER 7

DEATH OF THE REDS

FOR THREE DAYS, THERE HAD BEEN RUMORS THAT THE Braves were trying to work a deal for Boston reliever Jeff Reardon. Braves officials, however, weren't saying much, on or off the record. The Braves and Glavine were shelled 10-2 in the series finale in Philadelphia, and we flew to New York for a four-game set with the Mets. When I got off the plane, I found out the Reardon deal had been completed. The Braves had sent Richmond outfielder Sean Ross and Greenville pitcher Nate Minchey to the Red Sox in exchange for Reardon, who was the major leagues' all-time saves leader but no longer the dominant pitcher he once was. Still, he was a proven closer, something the Braves didn't have at the moment. And the deal had to be made before the end of the month, because players have to be on the roster before Sept. 1 to be eligible for the postseason.

While I was writing the Reardon story, I popped over to Shea Stadium to watch the Red and Mets play. This was the final straw for the Reds. They had a chance to cut the Braves' lead to five games, but Rob Dibble gave

This was the final straw for the Reds. They had a chance to cut the Braves' lead to five games.

up a three-run homer to Bonilla and they lost 4-3. Dibble, never the most stable individual in baseball, ripped off his jersey as he stalked off the field. It certainly appeared the Reds were done.

WEDNESDAY, SEPT. 2

Gotta love those Mets. On Tuesday, Vince Coleman got into an on-field shoving match with manager Jeff Torborg after arguing a called third strike, and drew a two-game suspension. Several players and coaches had to pull them apart. With this as backdrop, several players were talking about their most embarrassing moments. The best story belonged to Lemke.

"I was playing in [Class A] Durham and I was rounding third trying to score the winning run and the catcher was standing there. He lowered his shoulder into me and my false teeth popped out and hung up on the umpire's facemask. The ump also had tobacco juice all over his face. He handed [the false teeth] back to me and said, 'Thanks, but I've got my own.'"

More injury problems for the pitching staff. Pitching with a 4-0 lead in the fourth inning, Smoltz felt something pop in his groin. Instead of coming out, he tried to pitch with it. The Mets scored one run in the fourth, another in the fifth and four in the sixth and went on to win 6-5. Afterward, Smoltz asked me not to make a big deal of the injury. "I should have been able to pitch through it," he said. "Blame this one on me." That's typical Smoltz.

The loss, while it prevented a four-game sweep, didn't take any luster off the stay in New York. Nied, one of the players called up for the last month of the season, when teams are allowed to expand their rosters from 25 to 40, won his major-league debut in the third game, going seven innings and giving up just one run. The Mets hit several long fly balls off him, but each out seemed to add to his confidence. Justice had hit two home runs. And Reardon got two saves in three appearances.

The only negative, besides the one loss, was an injury suffered by Beauchamp, who slipped while getting off the bus at the hotel in Manhattan and banged up his knee. He would need surgery, but he told me that wouldn't be any worse than his experience going to the emergency room of a New York hospital. "I saw drug addicts and people who had been shot up," he said. "Now that was scary."

THURSDAY, SEPT. 3

No one likes makeup games. They cut into precious golf time. And this one was even worse than normal. It was against the Expos. This had all the earmarks of an excruciatingly painful exprience. And that's just what it turned out to be, as Montreal came to Atlanta for a day and put an 11-2 whipping on the Braves, chasing Leibrandt by the third inning. From the Braves' standpoint, the only positive to the day was that this was the final regular-season game against the Expos. The final tally was four wins, eight losses, 34 runs scored, 57 allowed.

New reliever Jeff Reardon picked up two saves in his first three appearances as a Brave.

Photo: DAVID TULIS

JONATHAN NEWTON

WEDNESDAY, SEPT. 9

The last trip to Atlanta for the Reds this season. Down by 7 1/2 games with only five left against the Braves, Cincinnati needed to sweep these two. But once again the spotlight was not on the division race, but on Sanders's continuing soap opera. Call it "All My Negotiations" or "Two Lives to Live." Remember all that talk about being fed up with the Falcons, about being a full-time Brave for the rest of the season? Well, forget it. Sanders was now trying to work a deal with the football team that would allow him to play this Sunday.

Without Sanders in the lineup, the Falcons had beaten the New York Jets in their opener, but not before they gave up a ton of passing yards. This only confirmed what everybody already knew: they needed him badly. So the Falcons and Sanders's agent, Parker, returned to the bargaining table. They hammered out a deal in which Sanders would get the $1 million bonus, and make close to $2 million total for the season. They also agreed to give him a "furlough" to play for the Braves exclusively during the postseason.

Schuerholz wasn't happy. He'd still have Sanders for the postseason, but by playing football, Sanders was exposing himself to a greater risk of injury. And there was a larger issue, larger even than the postseason roster. The expansion draft was coming up in Novem-

Bobby Cox and Charlie Leibrandt exchanged heated words on the mound when Cox removed the pitcher from a game in the fifth inning.

ENCORE!

ber, and the Braves could protect only 15 players from their entire organization. Sanders was young and had proved he could be an excellent baseball player. But where did his loyalties lie? Was there ever going to come a day when he gave up football to play baseball? Was he worth protecting? At this point, Schuerholz didn't have the answer to any of these questions. It would be another month before he would decide that protecting Sanders was the way to go.

On the field, it was a night for milestones. In a 12-7 win over the Reds, Glavine got his 20th win, Nixon stole his 300th career base and Lonnie Smith notched his 500th career RBI on a three-run homer in the first inning.

The next night, fans at the stadium hoisted brooms in celebration of a sweep. Sanders once again proved the value of a player with world-class speed when he scored the winning run by advancing from first to third after drawing a wild pickoff throw, then coming home on a sacrifice fly. With the 3-2 loss, the Reds fell 9 1/2 games behind the Braves. And they weren't even the second-place team anymore. The Padres had passed them.

FRIDAY, SEPT. 11

Ryan Klesko was called up today. The top prospect in the organization, Klesko was told the Braves wanted him to get some major-league at-bats, but the move may have been due as much to his sick mother. "She's probably still calling everyone," Klesko said. "Something like that really helps her." It's been a tough few months for Lorene Klesko. In August she was so sick that Klesko had to leave his team in Richmond and return to his home in Westminster, Calif. "My parents got divorced, and it was my mom that sent me to pitching and hitting camp," he said. "We're super close, and it got so bad that I had to go home." Klesko said his mother had become ill from inhaling chemicals at her place of work.

SUNDAY, SEPT. 13

The Braves completed a three-game sweep of the Astros, their seventh three-game sweep of the season and 14th sweep overall, as they've also taken five two-gamers and two four-gamers. It was also their ninth straight win, giving them seven streaks of five or more wins. The 53 wins that have made up the seven streaks account for 68 percent of their season total of 87 wins. In those games, they have outscored their opponents 279-111 and their ERA has been 1.89. They're the first team to take all nine games from the Astros in Houston.

MONDAY, SEPT. 14

On the off-day in Cincinnati, the Braves held their team party. Each player and coach got a gift from another one. Blauser got a football chin strap for his square jaw. Pendleton, who always seems to be hobbling, got a cane. Ned Yost, who dresses by the numbers, got a paint-by-numbers kit. Glavine, who is getting married after the sea-

In a 12-7 win over the Reds, Glavine got his 20th win, Nixon stole his 300th career base and Lonnie Smith notched his 500th career RBI on a three-run homer in the first inning.

son, got a pair of edible underwear. Lemke got a book on how to make love to women. "I'll keep it in my back pocket," he said.

The next day, a man walks into the clubhouse and passes out envelopes to all the players. They're from the city of Philadelphia, which wants every athlete who has played in that city to pay a wage tax for every day they spent there, going back to 1986. For maximum impact, the letters were timed to arrive on the same day. Attorneys and investigators combed through media guides, rosters and press reports to compile the list of potential taxpayers, even players who have retired. The Braves already pay wage taxes in five states — California, New York, Illinois, Minnesota and Missouri. But Philadelphia is the first city to do this. The tax is 6 percent of the prorated salary for every day the team is in town. That would mean that Glavine, who makes more than $2.9 million, would have to pay a tax bill of $6,122. The best comment came from Reds outfielder Bip Roberts, who said, "I'll pay it. I'm a young black man from Oakland. [If I don't,] they'll haul my butt to San Quentin."

That night, the Reds ended Atlanta's winning streak, 4-2.

WEDNESDAY, SEPT. 16

Stanton looked a little worn out. No wonder. After giving up the winning hit the previous night, he spent most of the day on the telephone with his wife Debbie, who just had a baby boy, William Mitchell. Stanton had planned on getting back for the birth, but they couldn't wait; the umbilical cord was wrapped around the baby's neck. He had to content himself with passing out cigars. A few hours later, the Braves beat the Reds 3-2 on an eighth-inning home run by Blauser. Pete Smith started, but guess who got the win? That's right, Stanton. No one was talking about the division lead in terms of games ahead anymore. Now the focus was the "magic number." That's the number of wins by the first-place team combined with losses by the second-place team that will clinch the division title. The Braves' magic number is down to eight.

THURSDAY, SEPT. 17

The Reds won the final game of the season between the two clubs 3-2, but the story of the day came out of the Cincinnati locker room after the game, when Piniella took a run at Dibble. Piniella had told reporters that Dibble told him his right shoulder had tightened before the game and he wouldn't be able to pitch. Cincinnati Post reporter Bill Peterson asked Dibble if this was true, and Dibble said no, Piniella was lying. Peterson went back to Piniella and relayed Dibble's message, and the manager then charged out of his office and tackled Dibble. After a few punches were thrown, they were pulled apart and the media was evicted from the clubhouse. I was already back at my seat in the press box when the Cincinnati reporters came running in, talking excitedly about the fight. I called my paper and was asked to write a short story. Problem was, I had to finish my game story in time to

Reds manager Lou Piniella charged out of his office and tackled Rob Dibble. After a few punches were thrown, they were pulled apart and the media was evicted from the clubhouse.

JONATHAN NEWTON

catch the charter flight home. So when I got on the bus I asked Nixon if I could use his cellular phone. When I got to the plane, I made the call and dictated a story to one of my editors.

FRIDAY, SEPT. 18

The Braves were back home to play the Astros, who showed a lot more talent on the road than they had at home. They thrashed the Braves 13-3, but that wasn't the worst news. Olson was out for the season. He had partially dislocated his right ankle and fractured his right fibula in a violent collision with Houston's Ken Caminiti in the fourth inning. Olson was in good spirits, tomahawk-chopping on the stretcher as he was being wheeled off the field. Trainer Dave Pursley went with him to the hospital.

"He's a little upset he'll miss pheasant hunting this year," Pursley reported later.

Olson's injury put a lot of pressure on Berryhill. The former Cub had done a good job offensively with 10 homers and 40 RBIs, but he had experienced some problems defensively. The Braves would now activate rookie Javier Lopez, who could be used behind the plate during the playoffs in an emergency. Plus, Cabrera could catch. But for now, Berryhill was The Man.

Sweep city: The Braves swept 14 series in 1992: five two-gamers, two four-gamers and seven three-gamers.

JONATHAN NEWTON

The Braves lost Greg Olson for the rest of the season when he dislocated his right ankle and fractured a fibula while being bowled over at home plate by Houston's Ken Caminiti.

After the injury, Greg Olson rejoined the Braves as a cast-wearing, crutches-bearing cheerleader.

FRANK NIEMER

ENCORE!

DAVID TULIS

SUNDAY, SEPT. 20

Take that, Astros. The magic number was now seven after a 16-1 trouncing of Houston in the season series finale. It was quite a feat for a team that had scored only 10 runs in the previous four games. The highlight was four Braves home runs in the sixth inning. Justice, Hunter and Gant homered in consecutive at-bats, only the second time an Atlanta club had performed that feat, then one out later Lemke added a fourth.

The Braves now had 132 homers for the season, the most in the league. It was a balanced long-ball attack, as Pendleton had 21 homers, Justice 18, Gant 16, Hunter 14 and Blauser 13.

Gant's homer almost caused a brawl. He had been upset that Astros reliever Al Osuna threw a ball under his chin, and when he hit the homer, he stopped to watch it before he began running. When he finally began moving, catcher Scooter Tucker began following him, and plate umpire Doug Harvey ran out to stop Tucker. When Gant crossed the plate, he and Tucker came nose to nose, but Harvey was able to brush Gant away.

"I did it on purpose," said Gant. "I don't do that if he doesn't brush me back. I said a few choice words, but it wasn't anything to fight about." Tucker, asked what he had said to Gant at the plate, said, "I sure wasn't congratulating him on his homer."

One day after the Astros knocked out Greg Olson, Atlanta's Brian Hunter flattened Scott Servais while trying to score.

THE 1992 ATLANTA BRAVES

Almost overlooked in all the offense was a milestone by Pendleton. His four RBIs gave him 100 for the season, making him the first Atlanta third baseman to reach that number since Darrell Evans did it in 1973.

MONDAY, SEPT. 21

Time for the last road trip of the season — two games apiece in both Los Angeles and San Francisco, followed by three in San Diego. The Braves beat the Dodgers in the opener 4-2 as Smith ran his record to 6-0. The next night, however, the Dodgers came back and beat the Braves 4-1. Something was wrong.

The race had been all but conceded since the final game in Houston eight days before. That victory had given the Braves a 10 1/2-game lead. But the Reds were staging a belated comeback, and the margin was down to 6 1/2. On the injury front, Merkcer's ribs were bothering him, and it was feared he might have to miss the rest of the season. He hadn't made this trip.

Dodger Stadium just wasn't the place it used to be. It hardly seemed possible that only a year ago the Dodgers were neck and neck with the Braves for the division title. Now here they were in last place, an astounding 29 1/2 games behind the Braves. Attendance was down, and the club was starting to pinch pennies. No longer were the stadium lights being turned on for batting practice. Desserts were no longer being served in the press dining room. Eight minor-league coaches, including Darrell Evans, had been let go, and they were folding their Gulf Coast League team. But to a reporter, the biggest indication of how far the Dodgers had fallen (bigger even than no desserts) was this: The Los Angeles Times was no longer sending a reporter on the road with the Dodgers. What have we come to?

WEDNESDAY, SEPT. 23

Leibrandt beat the Giants 7-0 for the Braves' 22nd shutout of the season, an Atlanta record. I spent some time talking with USA Today National League beat writer Rod Beaton and USA Today Baseball Weekly's Rob Rains about which managers were the most quotable. We all agreed that the best were Cincinnati's Piniella, Montreal's Alou and St. Louis's Joe Torre. The worst? Lasorda and Cox. Of Lasorda, Beaton said, "Even his own beat writers don't go to him." And how many times, he asked, could you listen to Lasorda talk about his playing days and how he lost playing time to Sandy Koufax? Of Cox, Rains said, "He's good to talk to in an informal setting, but doesn't seem comfortable criticizing his players or discussing strategy."

THURSDAY, SEPT. 24

Glavine, who had missed two starts because of his injured rib, came back but didn't look very good. He lasted just five innings and gave up four runs as the Braves were shut out by San Francisco 4-0. I got a call after the game from Dan Patrick of ESPN. I've known Patrick since he used to be the morning sports guy for 96 Rock. He

FRANK NIEMER

told me ESPN had taken a slow-motion clip of Glavine throwing a breaking ball to Will Clark earlier in the season, and compared it to a shot of one he threw to Clark today. It showed a significant difference in the break of the ball, today's hardly snapping at all. Glavine also appeared in today's tape to be having a hard time completing his delivery. Glavine wasn't impressed. "It's only a small adjustment," he said. "The thing is, I haven't pitched in a while, and it's not easy to flip the switch right back on." Privately, the Braves were concerned that Glavine might be physically worn down, as he was at the end of the 1991 season. They also were concerned about the Reds, who had won their eighth straight and knocked the lead down to 5 1/2 games.

Terry Pendleton became the first Braves third baseman to reach 100 RBIs since Darrel Evans did it in 1973.

FRIDAY, SEPT. 25

Before the opener of the three-game series with the Padres, I spent some time talking to Sheffield. When I told him I had an MVP vote, he found plenty of time to talk to me. He had spent most of the season flirting with the possibility of winning the triple crown, something no one had done since Boston's Carl Yastrzemski in 1967. But he felt it was unfair that he wasn't getting the attention in the MVP race that Pendleton and Bonds were. "I just don't understand that," he said. "I know that this team isn't going to win the division, but I want people to look at my numbers. Really, I think a lot more about the MVP than the triple crown." I don't think he'll get his wish, though. Voters tend to concentrate on the word "Valuable" in Most Valuable Player, and look for players on contending teams. Someone who plays for a team that doesn't win a championship has got to have significantly better stats than someone else on a title club. And Sheffield's numbers aren't that much better than those of Pendleton or Bonds, who are leading their clubs into the playoffs.

Because of the absence of Mercker, the Braves have promoted Pedro Borbon from Greenville. The name should be familiar. He's the son of former Big Red Machine reliever Pedro Borbon.

The Reds beat the Giants, and the Braves lost to the Padres 1-0. The lead was down to 4 1/2 games with nine to play. The Braves clubhouse was stone silent after the game. Cox had really gotten edgy, spending only a few seconds with reporters. "There are no ifs, ands or buts about it," said Nixon. "We've got to start doing something right now. If it takes a meeting every day, then so be it. We've got to make a move and see what happens, because it's getting way too close."

The Reds beat the Giants, and the Braves lost to the Padres 1-0. The lead was down to 4 1/2 games with nine to play.

CHAPTER 8

THE WEST IS WON

BEING ON THE WEST COAST WAS A BIG HELP ON THIS day. With their lead down to 4 1/2 games and the magic number at five, the Braves arrived at the stadium in San Diego and quickly learned that the Reds had lost to the Giants in Cincinnati. Cox's whole demeanor changed when he heard the score. "Now if we can win the next two games here, I can enjoy my day off," he said. They could, and he did. With the score tied 1-1 in the 10th, Blauser doubled off the left-field wall, then scored on a single by Lonnie Smith. The magic number was down to three. "I don't think you can put into words the importance of this game," said Blauser.

The next day, in the last road game of the season, the Braves again won in 10 innings, again by a 2-1 score. The Reds also won, but the magic number was down to two with seven games to play. For all practical purposes, it was over.

Monday was an off day, but I had another concern. While the team packed up and went home on the charter, I had to wait a couple of hours for my commercial flight. My wife was pregnant with twins, and getting close to delivery. She hadn't wanted me to go on this trip, but now I was only a few hours from being home.

I called Beth Ann before I got on the plane, and she

"I don't think you can put into words the importance of this game."

JEFF BLAUSER,
AFTER THE BRAVES BEAT
THE PADRES TO REDUCE
THEIR MAGIC NUMBER
TO THREE

said she felt fine. But when we got to Phoenix for a 45-minute lay-over, she told me she thought her water had broken. Yes, the babies were on their way. As she headed for Northside Hospital, I still had about three hours in the air. One of the flight attendants kept me company as everyone else slept, and gave me a couple of bottles of wine to take home. I finally made it to the hospital, and 45 minutes later had two little girls, Ashley and Lindsey. They were born one day before the Braves would clinch the West.

TUESDAY, SEPT. 29

Olson was back in the clubhouse. He had been prepared to fly to the West Coast if the Braves had clinched out there, but they saved him the trip. Now he was wearing a big cast and talking about all the attention he had received. He got a letter from Kasten's kids, some salmon paté from Ted and Jane, and Sen. Wyche Fowler came by to see him in the hospital. He was also excited about the prospect of again writing a postseason diary for the *Journal-Constitution*. He had been thinking about this all season, even coming up to me once to ask if I'd make sure we'd have him do the diary again if the club made the playoffs.

That issue was settled when the Braves beat the Giants 6-0 behind Leibrandt and the Reds lost to the Dodgers 5-0. *Constitution* colum-nist Steve Hummer described the feeling best when he wrote: "Whaddaya call it now? From Burst to First? From Best to Crest? From High Ground to One More Round? Nothing has quite the same 'peal, heh, as when these Braves did the worst to first thing one year ago."

Indeed. The Braves celebrated in the traditional manner, spraying each other with champagne and water in the clubhouse. TBS's Sutton was prepared, though, bringing a rain suit and golf hat to wear while he did champagne- and water-splashed interviews.

Cox was one of the last to leave the clubhouse. He looked like a new man. "Now we can rest up some," he said. "Now we don't have to worry about those damn Reds and can look to the playoffs. Boy, I'm glad it's over."

WEDNESDAY, SEPT. 30

With the final six games of the regular season a moot point, the big question on everyone's mind was what the pitching rotation would be for the playoffs against Pittsburgh. All five starters had good creden-tials. Glavine had 20 wins and a 2.82 ERA. Smoltz was 15-12, 2.89. Avery was 11-11, 3.20. Leibrandt was 14-7, 3.45, and Pete Smith was 6-0, 1.98. But most managers go with three-man rotations in the playoffs, and that likely would mean Leibrandt and Smith would be left out in the cold.

While working on the playoff pitching story before the game, I got a tip from *Constitution* columnist Mark Bradley, who had heard from a source that Glavine had been pitching with a broken rib. Glavine,

When the Braves returned from the West Coast, fans came to the stadium ready to celebrate another NL West championship.

Photo: RICH MAHAN

FRANK NIEMEIR

ENCORE!

JONATHAN NEWTON

*Party time:
Charlie Leibrandt
pitched a complete
game in the clincher,
touching off
celebrations around
town and in the
Braves locker room.*

FRANK NIEMEIR

THE 1992 ATLANTA BRAVES

each leading some offensive categories. I also felt neither the Braves nor the Pirates would have won their divisions without those players. So, since it was a tossup, I went with the player I had seen all season. The top five players on my ballot were Pendleton, Bonds, Sheffield, San Diego's Fred McGriff and Pittsburgh's Andy Van Slyke.

I was not swayed by a fax I got from Bonds's agent, who apparently sent one to all the MVP voters.

That night the Braves swept both games of the doubleheader, 4-1 and 7-2, and achieved a couple of milestones. The crowd of 41,075 for the second game put them over the 3 million mark, only the seventh club in major-league history to reach that goal. "To me," said Schuerholz, "that is a sign of how much this organization has come along, as much as our pennant and two division titles."

In the opener, Smoltz's three strikeouts gave him the league lead with 215. He could thank David Cone for the title. Cone had 214 strikeouts when he was traded to Toronto in late August. Cone's American League strikeouts could not count toward the NL title. In the second game, Pete Smith went 6 1/3 innings to become only the third Atlanta pitcher to win his first seven decisions, matching Larry McWilliams (1978) and Rick Mahler (1985). It was the Braves' third doubleheader sweep of the season, the first time they had done that since 1976.

SUNDAY, OCT. 4

After a 1-0 victory over the Padres in a game shortened by rain to six innings on Saturday, the Braves wrapped up the season by failing to hold onto a 3-0 lead. The Padres won 4-3 in 12 innings as Glavine watched what should have been his 21st victory fall victim to a shaky performance by the bullpen. He pitched five innings, allowing only one hit and no runs, and left with a 3-0 lead. But a bigger question was whether Pendleton would get his 200th hit. He singled on his first at-bat in the first inning for No. 199. In the second, he lined a ball up the middle, but it was picked off by Padres starter Doug Brocail. Pendleton grounded out to shortstop in the fifth, and came to the plate for the final time in the eighth. After fouling off a few pitches, he grounded to short. In the ninth, he came out of the game with the Braves leading 3-2. "Bobby asked me if I wanted to stay in the game and I said no," Pendleton said. "Then I was sitting with an ice pack in the training room and my teammates started ragging on me, saying, 'You're a bum.'" Justice hit his 21st homer, tying him with Pendleton for the team lead. The final record was 98-64.

MONDAY, OCT. 5

One day from the beginning of the National League Championship Series, a rematch between the Braves and Pirates. It was a day for asking questions. What would be the Braves' key to winning? Would it be Nixon, who had missed the playoffs last season because of his drug suspension? This season he had hit .400 with seven stolen

"To me, that is a sign of how much this organization has come along, as much as our pennant and two division titles."

JOHN SCHUERHOLZ, ON THE BRAVES' 1992 ATTENDANCE

bases against Pittsburgh, and he had a .313 career average vs. the Pirates. Would Bonds go into another postseason shell? In 3 postseason games over the two previous seasons, Bonds had managed just seven hits in 45 at-bats, with no home runs and one RBI. Could the Braves survive the loss of Olson, who was one of their best players in the '91 postseason? Were the Pirates jinxed in the playoffs after losing in the NLCS two years in a row?

The press conference was the typical day-before-the-series-begins affair, filled with cliches, banalities and platitudes. Glenn Sheeley, in his "Sportslite" column for the *Journal-Constitution,* wrote a tongue-in-cheek analysis of who got the better of it. Overall, he gave the edge to the Braves. Some of his other awards: Best willpower: Pittsburgh manager Jim Leyland, who went through the entire interview without a cigarette. "This is the same guy," he wrote, "that sneaks into the dugout tunnel during a game and lights up." Best excuse for being late to the press conference: The Pirates, who flew USAir, which went on strike that day.

JONATHAN NEWTON

Atlanta's media outlets were tripping over each other trying to line up players for "exclusive" reports. Justice was doing a daily spot for WAGA, which put Hullinger, the sports director, in an awkward position. Hullinger and I had spent much of the season doing spots on 96 Rock, both of us sometimes critical of Justice. Now Hullinger was doing a daily interview with him. Anything for ratings (or newspaper sales).

WSB-TV had Olson, who also was doing his diary for the *Journal-Constitution.* 96 Rock had Glavine. All of this made Blauser a little jealous. "Hey," he said in mock protest. "I'm not like Olson. I don't need the money."

Smoltz led the league with 215 strikeouts. David Cone had 214 strikeouts when he was traded to Toronto in late August.

CHAPTER 9

A DATE WITH STEELTOWN

TUESDAY, OCT. 6

T HE FEVER WAS DEFINITELY BACK. ATLANTA BAR OWNER Warren Bruno saw an ad in the *Journal-Constitution* from someone who wanted to trade his 150-pound, 16-foot-long tomahawk for World Series tickets. Bruno needed a tomahawk for his bar, so he made the swap, giving up four tickets to the sixth game of the World Series and two for the playoff opener.

There would be a full stadium for the opener, but it wouldn't include me. It was Yom Kippur, the most important of the Jewish holidays. Also missing would be Kasten. "I wouldn't be coming to the game if it was the seventh game of the World Series," he said.

Once again, Sanders was in the spotlight. He had a tentative plan to play for the Braves in the first four games, take a chartered jet to Miami and join the Falcons for their game with the Dolphins on Sunday afternoon, then fly back to Pittsburgh that night for Game 5, if it was necessary. "I don't think he's decided what he wants to do," said Parker, his agent. "But I wouldn't rule out anything with Deion. He might have to parachute into the stadium."

The Braves threw a body-block on Pirates slugger Barry Bonds for the second year in a row.

Photo: DAVID TULIS

Before the game, three Atlanta police dogs sniffed around the stadium for explosives. They concentrated heavily on the VIP boxes. "We're making sure nobody gets a chance to make a statement on national television," said officer J.A. Villafane.

Finally, they got down to the business of playing. It was all Atlanta in the opener, Smoltz shutting down Doug Drabek and the Pirates 5-1. It was the same score, only reversed, as the 1991 NLCS opener. Blauser homered, and Bream and Lemke each had two hits. Smoltz went a strong eight innings, and Stanton finished up in the ninth. The defense was highlighted by a snappy 5-4-3 double play that Pendleton initiated by gloving a Jay Bell smash to third.

"That's one of the reasons why they're so good," said Leyland. "You don't get many opportunities against that pitching staff. Any lee-way at all, with all that pitching, they're going to bury you."

The *Journal-Constitution*, trying to get the fans involved (and sell more newspapers), set up a phone line for headline suggestions. If the editors saw one they liked better than anything they had, they used it, and credited the reader who called it in. "Holy Smoltz," suggested by reader Theresa Hermann of Kennesaw, was used on page A1. Frankly, I liked the whole concept of readers writing headlines. I eagerly awaited its logical conclusion, when readers would write the game stories. Me? I'd become an editor. Make life miserable for someone else for a change. (Just kidding, boss.)

WEDNESDAY, OCT. 7

My favorite day of the postseason. Why? Because it's the only afternoon game the Braves will play. Night baseball may be good for TV ratings, but it stinks for almost everyone else. The games don't start until 8:30, and sometimes don't end until after midnight. Kids can't stay up because they have to go to school; adults can, but probably shouldn't, considering the shape they're in the next morning; reporters have to scramble furiously to make deadline; and a lot of morning newspapers have only sketchy coverage because the games ended too late for many stories to make the home-delivered editions. Other than that, I'm all in favor of night baseball.

Early Wednesday, a woman named Debbie Avery (no relation to Steve, she said) called the paper and said she had just had a conversation with Bonds, who was driving through her neighborhood looking for real estate. She said a cranberry-colored Lincoln Continental pulled up in front of her house, and a man rolled down the window and said, "Hi, I'm Barry Bonds. I play ball with the Pirates and I'm looking for a good-sized house with a lot of land." She said she and Bonds "spoke for about 15 minutes about the pros and cons of living close to the city." I knew Bonds was interested in possibly joining the Braves as a free agent next season, but I couldn't believe he'd go house-hunting during the playoffs. I had to ask him about it, but I had to get him alone, because the *Journal-Constitution* had this story by itself. Finally, after Bonds had three sessions with large groups of

Before Game 1, three Atlanta police dogs sniffed around the stadium for explosives. They concentrated heavily on the VIP boxes.

JONATHAN NEWTON

RICH MAHAN

*Game 1: Not much went
right for the Pirates, who
were shut down on five hits
by John Smoltz and
Mike Stanton.*

RICH MAHAN

reporters, I caught him on his way to getting his bat for batting practice. He acknowledged the story, saying he had done the same thing in several other cities, including Chicago and New York. Nixon also told me that Bonds had spoken with him about good places to live in Atlanta. When I told this to Pirates general manager Ted Simmons, he seemed resigned. "I might do the same thing if I were in his shoes," he said. "His circumstances are very unusual and very enviable." Schuerholz smirked and said, "Shoot, I've been looking for a house here for two years."

Schuerholz wasn't as glib on another subject — Sanders. He'd been doing a good job of making it appear the whole Sanders baseball/football scenario didn't bother him, but he was starting to slip in that regard. "A lot of people make a big deal about this guy," he said. "I'm not. No individual is more important than this team. This team has worked too hard to get here, and nothing is going to get in the way of that. We were told that he would be full-time with us."

"We want 25 guys here," said Cox. "We don't want to play without one. I don't know where his obligations lie."

Sanders wasn't talking, but Nixon told me there wasn't any question about what he'd do. "He's going," Nixon said. "He has to think about his family." His family? Well, there was the matter of Sanders giving up a game check from the Falcons if he missed the Miami game. That would cost him about $116,000.

Down in Turner's box beside the Braves' dugout, the subject was politics. Sitting with Ted and Jane were Georgia Gov. Zell Miller, Sen. Wyche Fowler, Reps. Newt Gingrich, Buddy Darden and John Lewis, Fulton County Commission chairman Michael Lomax and Atlanta City Council president Marvin Arrington. Oh, yes, and former president Jimmy Carter and his wife, Rosalyn. It was so crowded, no wonder Turner didn't recognize Falcons quarterback Chris Miller.

It wasn't much of a game — unless you were a Braves fan. Then the 13-5 rout was pure heaven, highlighted by Gant's fifth-inning grand slam. Every starter except Avery got a hit.

Avery, meanwhile, extended his streak of consecutive scoreless innings in the NL playoffs to 22 1/3 — all against the Pirates. He pitched six shutout innings before the Pirates reached him for four runs in the seventh. Pirates starter Danny Jackson, who came into the game with a lifetime 3-1 record in the postseason, lasted only five outs, giving up four runs. With a 2-0 lead in games, the talk in the stands was about a four-game sweep. But not in the clubhouse. "If you're expecting them to role over and concede," warned Blauser, "they won't." Smart guy, that Blauser.

Game 2: Ron Gant provided the big blow, a grand slam in the fifth inning, as the Braves romped 13-5.

W. A. BRIDGES JR.

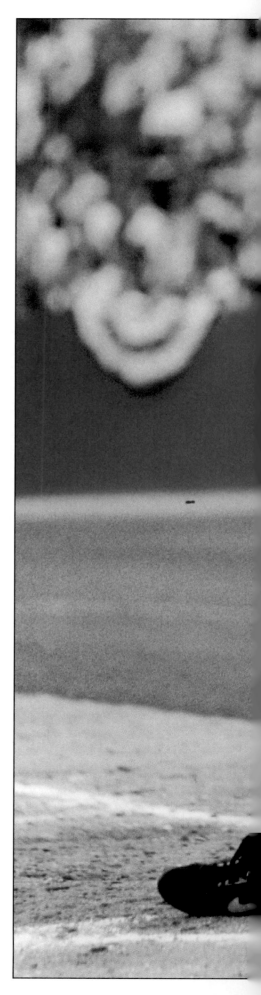

148

Game 2:
A rare joy of postseason baseball — an afternoon game in the sunshine and shadows at Atlanta-Fulton County Stadium.

JONATHAN NEWTON

*Game 2:
Barry Bonds's
postseason struggles
continued as he
struck out against
Steve Avery.*

JONATHAN NEWTON

THURSDAY, OCT. 8

There was only one thing wrong with all the talk about a sweep. To accomplish it, the Braves would have to beat the knuckleballer, Wakefield, in Game 3. Based on how he'd handcuffed them back in August, there was no reason to think they'd handle him any better now. With that thought in mind, the Braves decided to have the club hit against a knuckleballer in batting practice. So for the off-day workout at Three Rivers Stadium, Schuerholz brought in Bruce Dal Canton, a former major-league knuckleballer who was now the Braves' pitching coach at Richmond and who lived just 15 minutes from Three Rivers in a Pittsburgh suburb. "I was sitting home watching a game when John called," Dal Canton said. "I really never thought about the possibility of that happening." There was plenty of laughing and joking during the 20-minute hitting session, but one thing wasn't very funny. Almost no one could hit Dal Canton. Only Justice was able to put the ball in the seats off him.

Wakefield, of course, was the big story of the off-day. His was a great story even without the backdrop of the playoffs. He was an eighth-round pick out of Florida Tech in 1988 as an infielder, but hit just .189 in his first full season in the minors. The Pirates were ready to release him, but he agreed to go to the instructional league as a pitcher. He learned how to throw the knuckler, a pitch that bobs and weaves all over the place because it has no spin to stabilize it. When Pirates pitchers Zane Smith and Bob Walk went down with injuries this season, Wakefield was brought up to Pittsburgh. In 13 starts, he was 8-1 with a 2.15 ERA. Obviously, the Braves weren't the only team that couldn't hit him.

FRIDAY, OCT. 9

There was no news in Pittsburgh. Or rather, no newspapers. The two local papers, the *Press* and the *Post-Gazette,* have been sidelined for five months by a Teamsters strike. The *Post-Gazette* was distributing a five-page fax newspaper to subscribing businesses, and the *Press* was mailing a paper called the *Allegheny Bulletin* to subscribers three times a week. It had a sports section only two times a week, however. But the most innovative way of spreading the news was developed by the *Post-Gazette,* which dispatched two town criers in colonial garb — including black three-cornered hats over white ponytailed wigs — to cry out the news through a megaphone.

"This is the most awkward time of my journalism career," said Russ Brown, the *Press's* assistant managing editor for sports. "The Steelers have a new head coach and have entered a new era. The Penguins repeated as NHL Stanley Cup champions. And high school football is big in this area. There is so much going on. We couldn't have picked a more frustrating time to be out of work."

Another disappointment is missing Hertzel's baseball writing for the *Press.* He is truly one of the best, and one of the few old-timers remaining on the beat.

Preparing to face knuckleballer Tim Wakefield in Game 3, the Braves brought in Bruce Dal Canton to pitch batting practice. He lived just 15 minutes from Three Rivers Stadium.

DAVID TULIS

Before the game, Leyland announced that if the series went that far, Walk, not Jackson, would start Game 5. That wasn't surprising in light of Jackson's poor showing in Game 2. On the Braves' side, Smoltz, the scheduled Game 4 pitcher, said his back had stiffened and was giving him some trouble, although he expected to be able to pitch.

That was good news for the Braves, because Wakefield cut the Pirates' deficit in half with a 3-2 win.

"It's frustrating we didn't come out with a win," said Blauser. "Tip your hat to Wakefield. I thought we looked a lot better this time against him. They made some good plays."

The Braves got just five hits off Wakefield, including solo home runs by Bream and Gant. For most of the night, they looked like they were swatting flies. "It was exciting to finally have a dream come true," said Wakefield. "A rookie taking part in the League Championship Series. I'm not an emotional person, but I may never have that chance again."

Wakefield may have baffled the Braves, but he inspired the readers who called in headline suggestions. They ranged from "Wake-fields of Dreams" to my favorite, "Wakefield is a knucklehead."

The victim of the Cinderella story was Glavine, for whom the feeling was familiar. The loss dropped him to 0-3 lifetime in the playoffs,

Game 3: Things were glum on the Atlanta bench as Tim Wakefield baffled the Braves hitters with his knuckler.

coming on top of two defeats by the Pirates last October. But he wasn't discouraged over his performance; he had allowed three runs in 6 1/3 innings. Stanton had let the third run score on a fly ball in the seventh, but it was charged to Glavine because he had put the runner on by giving up a single. "As far as I'm concerned," said Glavine, "if I can get to the seventh and give up only three runs, I've done my job. Things just haven't worked out for me."

The Braves were still in command with a 2-1 lead, but they had to be concerned about Wakefield. All the Pirates needed was a split of the next two games in Pittsburgh to send the series back to Atlanta for Game 6, where the Braves would have to face Wakefield again. If they lost to him again, everything would come down to Game 7. No one wanted to stake the entire season on one game if they didn't have to.

"Let's put this one away the next two nights so we don't have to see this guy again," said Nixon.

If only it were that easy.

SATURDAY, OCT. 10

Say what you will about Sanders, but give him credit for this: the guy can flat fill up newspaper space. Today it was Deion and the Angry Call From Kasten. The Braves president, who always had been fond of Sanders, called him at the player's hotel room to ask if Sanders really intended to play football Sunday. Sanders told him yes, which was not the answer Kasten wanted to hear. The rest of the conversation was not fit for a family newspaper. Sanders slammed the phone down on Kasten. Sanders's teammates, however, didn't seem to be bothered at all by what he was doing. "We understand the business side of it," said Lemke.

In contrast to the players' attitude was that of CBS announcers Sean McDonough and Tim McCarver. "Deion is doing a self-centered thing," McDonough told his audience. "The guy is playing both ends against the middle," said McCarver. "They talk about him being the consummate team player, but if he plays football, what kind of shape will he be in to play baseball? Why should the income from a shoe contract take allegiance over the baseball team? The way I see that, it's flat wrong."

Smoltz was obviously in pain. His back had been worked on before the game by a chiropractor. But he felt he could endure the pain, and he was right. He went 6 1/3 innings, giving up four runs, but it was enough as the Braves won 6-4 to take a 3-1 lead in games. With the Braves trailing 3-2 in the fifth, Justice singled home Nixon to tie it, and Blauser scored the go-ahead run on a fielder's choice by Hunter when the throw home by third baseman Jeff King pulled Pittsburgh catcher Mike LaValliere off the plate. The Braves added two more in the sixth when Nixon doubled home Smoltz and Blauser singled in Nixon. The Pirates could manage only one more run, Van Slyke doubling home Alex Cole in the seventh.

Nixon had four hits and two RBIs. It was important to him to con-

Stan Kasten called Deion Sanders to ask if he really intended to play football Sunday afternoon in Miami, then fly to Pittsburgh for Game 5 on Sunday night. Sanders told him yes. The rest of the conversation was not fit for a family newspaper.

FRANK NIEMEIR

"There is no one here who wants to win more than I do. No one can really know how I feel inside after what I went through last season."

OTIS NIXON,
WHO MISSED
THE '91 PLAYOFFS
BECAUSE OF A
DRUG SUSPENSION,
AFTER GOING
4-FOR-4 IN GAME 4

JONATHAN NEWTON

THE 1992 ATLANTA BRAVES

tribute as much as possible. Missing the '91 postseason still gnawed at him. "There is no one here who wants to win more than I do," he said. "No one can really know how I feel inside after what I went through last season."

Smoltz wasn't as dominating as he had been in the opener, walking four batters in the first three innings. But he struck out nine and kept the Braves in the game until the offense took over. Stanton came on in the seventh after Van Slyke's double, and with the tying run at the plate, struck out Bonds and got King to ground out. Stanton then pitched a perfect eighth before Reardon nailed it down in the ninth for the Braves' first save of the postseason.

Now all that stood between the Braves and the World Series was Walk, who in 10 years was 5-9 with a 4.95 ERA against Atlanta. He was a huge underdog against Avery.

Figuring the series wouldn't go back to Atlanta, many of the sportswriters changed their airline reservations, making plans to go home for a few days. If Avery and the Braves won, they'd have a whole week before the Series started.

SUNDAY, OCT. 11

Pre-game batting practice was rained out, which made it difficult for the reporters to get notes, because the players remained in the clubhouse, where the media are not allowed before the game. With no players to talk to, I struck up a conversation with McCarver. The topic? What else? Sanders and today's two-sport adventure. "Ridiculous," McCarver snorted. "This team is trying to get to a World Series and this guy is worried about his wallet."

Sanders was furious about all the heat he was taking on CBS. He still wasn't talking to Atlanta reporters, but that didn't stop Chambers from calling the *Journal-Constitution* office to complain.

"How can a person giving himself between two teams be self-centered?" she asked. "People don't know how tired he is when he gets home. He's so exhausted, he doesn't want to eat. But he still doesn't neglect me or his daughter. He still gets up in the morning to take his daughter to school when he could be getting another two or three hours of sleep. That's the part the media doesn't see."

Sanders, meanwhile, was on his way back from Miami, where, in addition to his regular cornerback duties, he had returned two kickoffs and one punt, and played two snaps on offense as a wide receiver (catching one pass for nine yards). None of that, however, was enough to prevent the Falcons from losing to the Dolphins 21-17. "He looks like a piece of you-know-what warmed over," said Falcons teammate Andre Rison. "But this is something Deion wanted to do, and he set his mind to it. How many chances do you get to put yourself in the record books like this one?"

But at what cost? Sanders needed two bags of intravenous fluids before Falcons trainers would allow him to leave Joe Robbie Stadium. And when he did leave, he was limping badly.

"People don't know how tired he is when he gets home. He's so exhausted, he doesn't want to eat. But he still gets up in the morning to take his daughter to school when he could be getting another two or three hours of sleep. That's the part the media doesn't see."

CAROLYN CHAMBERS, ANSWERING CRITICISM OF DEION SANDERS FOR PLAYING FOR THE FALCONS AND BRAVES ON THE SAME DAY

DAVID TULIS

*Game 5:
Bob Walk, a former
Brave whose repertoire
included mainly
breaking pitches,
shut the Braves down
on three hits.
The complete game
was only his second
since 1990.*

He returned to Three Rivers Stadium just a few minutes before the first pitch. A CBS crew, including announcer Pat O'Brien, had accompanied him on the jet, which Nike reportedly had paid for. Sanders spent the game bundled up in a parka on the bench. The word was that Cox was not going to use him unless he had to emtpy his bench.

For all his efforts, Sanders ended up a two-time loser when the Braves and Avery were shocked by the Pirates and Walk 7-1. Bonds finally came out of his postseason hibernation with two hits and an RBI. Avery didn't last the first inning, giving up four runs on five hits and getting just one out.

Walk, 35, a former Brave whose repertoire included mainly breaking pitches, shut the Braves down on three hits. The complete game was only his second since 1990. Of course, it didn't hurt that he was given a four-run lead in the first inning. "I'm not saying he didn't pitch a good game," said Nixon, "but the lead gave him some momentum."

The Braves were more concerned about Bonds, however. The night before he had met privately with Leyland in what the manager described as a "father-son chat." Bonds drove home a run in the first with a double, singled and scored in the third and saved a run in the fourth with a great catch in left field.

The victory left the Pirates in the same position the Braves had been in in '91 — down 3-2 with two games left on the road. They were acutely aware that Atlanta had managed to dig itself out of that

W. A. BRIDGES JR.

hole. They also knew that with Wakefield going in Game 6, they were likely to survive to a seventh game. "Can Atlanta win one game? Yes," said Leyland. "Can the Pirates win two? Yes."

MONDAY, OCT. 12

The final off-day of the series. The Braves put in a call to Phil Niekro to see if he could pitch batting practice before Game 6. Niekro is, after all, the most famous knuckleball pitcher in baseball history, not to mention a former Brave. They reached him at his parents' home in California. "I'd love to do it," he said, "They just have to get me home."

Niekro said he'd give the Braves some advice on how to hit the knuckler, but wouldn't tell me what it was. He didn't want the Pirates to see it in the paper.

The Braves didn't work out, but on the scoreboard at Atlanta-Fulton County Stadium they left a not-too-subtle message for the Pirates. It was the linescore from Game 2, the 13-5 Braves win. But hardly anyone noticed. The Pirates' workout consisted of two players running in the outfield.

Before Game 6, Phil Niekro said he'd give the Braves some advice on how to hit the knuckler, but wouldn't tell me what it was. He didn't want the Pirates to see it in the paper.

The Braves were beginning to show signs of tightness. Glavine wasn't calling 96 Rock anymore. He wanted $1,000 a call, but the station, which had been paying him through an ad package with a stereo chain, Hi-Fi Buys, said no. Blauser thought there was too much talk about Wakefield. He felt the players had "psyched themselves out about the guy."

Before Game 6, Nixon urged me to talk to Sanders. He said his teammate was upset about all the negative publicity. I declined. Sanders had spent the better part of the year refusing to talk to me or anyone else in the local press. Now he felt he needed us, and figured we'd come running to him. It wasn't going to happen.

He'd tried to pull this trick before, on Pasquarelli, the *Journal-Constitution's* Falcons reporter. He sent a Falcons gofer to tell Pasquarelli he wanted to talk. Pasquarelli said he'd be glad to talk, as long as Sanders answered specific questions. But Sanders only wanted to issue a statement. Forget it, Pasquarelli said.

In his attempts to play the Braves and Falcons off of each other in contract negotiations, Sanders claimed that the money in his Nike deal would not be affected by his giving up one sport. That, however, was not what a source inside Nike told Pasquarelli. The deal, the source said, was for $1 million a year over three years for playing two sports. It provided for substantial cuts if Sanders gave up either sport, the contract dropping to $100,000 a year. The situation would only get worse for Sanders in the game when he came up to pinch hit in the sixth inning and was roundly booed.

Niekro pitched batting practice, but from the crowd of reporters who queued up behind the cage, you would have thought it was Madonna out there. When he finished, Dal Canton took over. Again the Braves had trouble with him. They'd hit Niekro better, but he had basially just lobbed the ball in to them. "I didn't want to be a bigger part of their problem," he said.

As events unfolded, he needn't have worried. No one was going to be a bigger part of their problem on this night than Wakefield. Unless it was the Pirate hitters. They pounded Glavine and Freeman, and came away with a 13-4 victory. It was an unprecedented surrender of offense by the Braves, who in 19 previous postseason games over the past two years had not given up more than five runs in a game.

Wakefield wasn't as sharp as he'd been in Game 3, but he had a lot bigger margin for error. Glavine got turned inside-out, giving up a League Championship Series-record eight runs in the second inning without getting anyone out.

"It sure takes a lot of pressure off the catcher when you have an 8-0 lead and a knuckleballer pitching," said Pirates catcher Don Slaught.

Glavine, now 1-5 in the postseason, was heartbroken. "I stunk," he said. "My location wasn't very good. When I made decent pitches they hit the ball where (the Braves' fielders) weren't, and when I made

*Game 6:
"When I made decent pitches they hit the ball where we weren't, and when I made mistakes they hit them over the fence."*

TOM GLAVINE,
ON HIS PERFORMANCE
IN THE BRAVES' 13-4 LOSS

DAVID TULIS

Game 6:
Barry Bonds started
the damage, hitting
his first homer in
62 playoff at-bats
in the second inning,
and Tim Wakefield
again kept the Braves
off-balance.

RICH MAHAN

162

W. A. BRIDGES JR.

mistakes they hit them over the fence." Again it was Bonds who started the damage, hitting his first homer in 62 at-bats in the second inning. Even Cox, who never seems to feel he's out of a game, raised the white flag in the bottom of the second when, with runners at first and second and two outs, he let Leibrandt hit for himself.

Now the teams were tied 3-3. But the Braves were faced with the possibility of carving an ignominious place for themselves in baseball history: the first National League team to blow a 3-1 lead in the playoffs. It was startling how the two clubs had exchanged roles in the last two games. In the first four games of the series the Braves had been the aggressors, outscoring the Pirates 26-13. But in Games 5 and 6, the Pirates had scored 20 runs, 12 of them in the first two innings.

The Pirates definitely had the momenum, if you believed in such a thing. Leyland didn't. "There is no such thing as momentum in baseball," he said. "Momentum is just your next day's starting pitcher."

That was the one ray of sunshine for the Braves. The Game 7 matchup was Smoltz vs. Drabek. Atlanta was already 2-0 when those two had faced each other. Cox's decision to set up the rotation so Smoltz could pitch three times was looking like a pretty good move.

RICH MAHAN

*Game 6:
It didn't take long
for Braves fans to
realize this would be
a long night.*

Smoltz was tired. This would be his second start on three days' rest, and he had gone a total of 14 innings in his two previous NLCS starts. Oddly, because Drabek had been less effective than Smoltz, he was better rested. He had gone only a total of nine innings.

Still, Smoltz was the guy the Braves wanted in there with everything on the line. He had the talent, and, thanks to Llewellyn's help, the mental toughness, too. On a staff as deep and talented as the Braves' was, every pitcher had to carve out a special niche for himself. Smoltz's was this: money pitcher.

Before the game, Cox called everyone together for a meeting. A strange thing happened. The only player to stand up and talk was Justice. According to several of his teammates, everyone was shocked. Justice wasn't a team leader type; he'd never pretended to be. But here he was, speaking from the heart. And because he so rarely did this sort of thing, his words made an indelible impression on his teammates.

For eight innings, though, it appeared that Justice's emotional appeal would go unanswered. Smoltz was sharp, but Drabek was sharper.

The Pirates scored in the first when Orlando Merced knocked in Cole with a sacrifice fly, and they added another run in the sixth when Van Slyke singled Bell in from second. The Braves had a chance to tie it in the bottom of the sixth when they loaded the bases with nobody out, but came up with nothing after Blauser lined into a double play and Pendleton flied out to left. In the seventh they had runners at first and second with one out but couldn't capitalize when both Berryhill and Lonnie Smith hit lazy flyballs.

Then came an inning that will forever be remembered.

When the Braves came off the field after Reardon retired the Pirates in the top of the ninth (Smoltz had come out for a pinch hitter after the sixth and had been followed by Stanton, Pete Smith, Avery and Reardon), everyone felt they still had a chance, Nixon said.

"We had done it so many times before. It was kind of weird," he said. "We had been so down the last three games, the Pirates looked like they couldn't be beaten. But for some reason, suddenly, there was some life."

Drabek's pitch count was already into the 120s, and he appeared to be tiring, but surely the adrenaline from being three outs away from the World Series would sustain him. The Braves had the heart of their order coming up, the Nos. 3-4-5 batters, Pendleton, Justice and Bream. Pendleton, however, was batting only .231 in the series, and the switch hitter was only 1-for-21 left-handed, which was how he would face the right-handed Drabek. He was 0-for-3 on the night.

But this was a series that had rarely gone according to form. So Pendleton drilled a 1-and-1 pitch into the right-field corner for a double, and it was as if someone had flipped the crowd's "on" switch. The tomahawk chops and chanting began, and people rose to their

Game 7: For eight innings, it appeared that David Justice's emotional appeal would go unanswered. John Smoltz was sharp, but Doug Drabek was sharper.

FRANK NIEMEIR

feet. Justice followed with a ground ball to second that figured to get Pendleton to third at the cost of one out. The Pirates could afford to give up one run, as long as they left the bases cleared thereafter. Once again, fate stepped in. Pittsburgh second baseman Jose Lind, who had made just six errors all season, mishandled the ball, leaving Justice safe at first on the error and Pendleton at third. The roars grew louder, turning into a rhythmic chant of "Sid! Sid! Sid!" as Bream strode to the plate. Drabek, who had walked only one batter all night, walked Bream on four pitches, loading the bases. Now you couldn't hear yourself think.

That was it for Drabek. Leyland called for Stan Belinda. Gant was up next, and he took the breath out of the crowd on Belinda's second pitch with a drive to deep left field. He didn't quite get all of it, though, and Bonds caught it with his back almost up against the fence. Pendleton raced home. It was 2-1. There was only one out.

Up next, Berryhill. When he had taken over full time for the injured Olson late in the season, it was his defense, not his offense, that had been questioned. But in the playoffs, he was hitting just .143 (3-for-21). Belinda wasn't taking any chances, though, not with the tying run on second. He went to 3-and-1, then threw what he and LaValliere both thought was a strike. It wasn't. The bases were loaded again.

Game 7: Ted Turner's worry beads got a workout as the tension mounted.

Belliard was due up next, but there was no way he was going to hit. He was the Braves' smallest player and weakest hitter, and it was unlikely he'd be able to produce a fly ball deep enough to get Justice home. Belliard's sole role on this team was to provide excellent defense. They had no complaints about him in the field. He had been the starting shortstop in '91 and early '92, but had lost the job to Blauser. He was in the game now as a replacement at second base for Lemke, who had gone out for a pinch hitter in the seventh.

Out of the dugout came Hunter. Cox probably would have preferred a left-handed hitter against the right-handed Belinda, but he was out of them. All things considered, he was blessed to have a part-time starter like Hunter available as his fourth pinch hitter of the night.

Hunter lifted a soft fly ball into short right-center field, and for a moment it appeared it might drop in for a hit and score Justice, but Lind, backpedaling, caught it. You could see the sighs of relief on the Pittsburgh bench. One more out and the pennant was theirs.

With Reardon due up next, Cox once again reached into his bag of pinch hitters. He had two left, both catchers who had spent most of the season in the minors. But Javier Lopez was a 21-year-old with 16 career major-league at-bats, all this season after he'd been brought up from AA Greenville. Francisco "Frankie" Cabrera was four years older and had 252 more major-league at-bats. He'd been with AAA Richmond most of this season, but he'd done time in the majors in '89, '90, '91 and '92. He'd even had one of the biggest hits of the '91 season, a two-out, game-tying three-run homer off Cincinnati's Rob Dibble in the ninth inning of an August game the Braves eventually won.

There was no decision to make; it was Cabrera all the way. He wasn't nervous, he said later, just a little sore from having cracked his head on the dugout ceiling when he jumped up in excitement after Lind muffed Justice's grounder.

When Hunter went up to hit, Cabrera knew he was next. He told Hunter to "get on base and I was just going to try to hit a fly ball to score a run." When Hunter flied out, Cabrera had to go to Plan B. "I was thinking two out and I'm going to have to get a hit," he said.

Belinda immediately put himself in a 2-0 hole, missing the plate with his first two pitches. Now he had to throw a fastball and get it over the plate. He did, and Cabrera lashed it toward the left-field corner . . . but foul. The 2-1 pitch was another fastball. Cabrera swung. The ball shot off his bat, in the description of Journal-Constitution columnist Lewis Grizzard, "like a dog with turpentine on its hindparts" into left field. Justice scored. Bonds, a Gold Glove outfielder with a strong arm, picked up the ball. Bream, who Bradley said "runs as if pulling a team of mules behind him," rounded third, waved on by coach Jimy Williams.

Bonds's arm vs. Bream's legs. Extra innings for sure.

In the Braves dugout, Olson was jumping up and down on his

WILLIAM BERRY

good leg, yelling "Score! Score! Score!" Glavine was exhorting, "Sid, run like hell! Please, Sid!" Pendleton, too: "Let's go, baby," he shouted. "Feet don't fail me now. Bring it home, baby. Bring it home!"

At this moment, frozen in time as Bonds's right arm flashed with the throw to the plate that surely would overtake Bream, a question flashed in the minds of many. Why didn't Cox pinch-run for Bream? The answer was that Cox was thinking about his defensive alignment if the game went into extra innings, which seemed a distinct possibility. When Hunter hit for Belliard, Cox was out of second basemen. He would have had to move Pendleton to second and shift Gant to third, where he used to play before being turned into an outfielder. Hunter would have replaced Gant in left and Cabrera would have gone to first. Having four people playing out of position didn't seem to Cox like the way to win an extra-inning game. No, he'd take his chances with Bream's surgically repaired knees.

Bream certainly wasn't thinking about any of this as he lumbered toward the plate and a probable collison with his old Pirates teammate, LaValliere. But when these concerns were presented to him

Game 7: The 2-1 pitch was another fastball. Francisco Cabrera swung. The ball shot off his bat "like a dog with turpentine on its hindparts" into left field.

THE 1992 ATLANTA BRAVES

167

LOUIE FAVORITE

ENCORE!

So when the Braves pulled off their comeback, the winning hit coming at 11:53 p.m., you could hear a collective "Darn!" (or something similar) from the press box, as hundreds of reporters killed their Pirates-win leads and furiously scrambled to describe the Braves' miracle finish. I had approximately 45 seconds to get my first-edition story in, but worse, I had only another half-hour to get the second-edition story done, complete with quotes, for the paper that would be home-delivered to most of our subscribers. At that moment, I thought wistfully about looking for a job on the West Coast, where it was only 9 o'clock.

My deadline worries were petty, however, compared to what John Holland and his crew were facing. The Braves' visiting clubhouse manager had prepared the Pittsburgh locker room for a victory celebration, and he had to tear it all down before the Pirates returned from the field. Holland was in the clubhouse watching on television when Bream crossed the plate with the winning run. Immediately, he ordered his assistants into action.

They tore down the plastic that lined the lockers to protect the players' clothes from sprayed champagne. They took down the podium that had been set up in the center of the room for the trophy presentation. They unplugged cables and rolled cameras away. They took the champagne, packed it onto a cart and raced it through the stadium tunnel to the Braves' locker room.

I'm still not sure if I made my deadline (all I know is that my story was in the paper the next morning), but Holland made his. When the teary-eyed Pirates trudged into their clubhouse, there was no trace of what the room had looked like just five minutes before.

Leyland was far too distraught to worry about anyone's deadline. There were only six reporters in the Pirates clubhouse, but he felt there hadn't been a sufficient mourning period, and threw them out. He was escorted to a separate interview room, where he gamely tried to compose himself. "I'm still in shock," he said. "I felt the game was ours in the ninth after two outs. It's tough to lose [in the playoffs] like this three years in a row. I don't know how I'm going to handle it."

After finishing the interview, Leyland returned to the locker room. Or tried to return. The door was locked. What a night. He'd just suffered the most emotional loss of his career, and now he was locked out of his own clubhouse.

Finally, the door opened. The players looked like the survivors of a bomb blast. Walk was sitting on a table in the middle of the room, staring into space. Bonds was fetally curled in front of his locker. Lind ran for the trainer's room, off-limits to the reporters. *Boston Globe* columnist Michael Madden said the scene reminded him of the sixth game of the 1986 World Series, when the Red Sox, one out from the championship, blew the game (and eventually the Series) to the New York Mets.

The Braves' clubhouse looked like something out of one of those "Victory at Sea" videotapes. All that was missing was Cox putting on

John Holland, the visiting clubhouse manager, had prepared the Pittsburgh locker room for a victory celebration. He had to tear it all down before the Pirates returned from the field and move it all to the Braves' locker room.

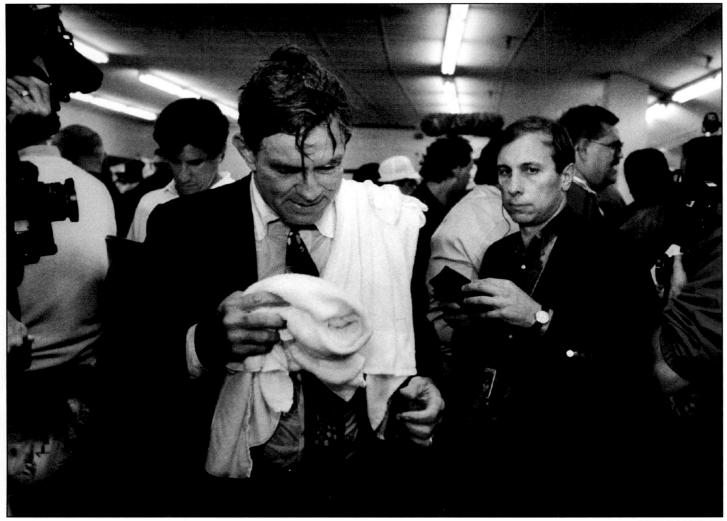

WILLIAM BERRY

a rain slicker and lashing himself to a mast. Water and champagne were spraying everywhere. Although this was typical locker-room behavior for a team winning a championship, what followed wasn't. McCarver was in the room to do postgame interviews. Sanders hadn't forgotten how McCarver had criticized him, and he planned to get even. He filled a plastic tub with water, and when he found McCarver, he dumped the water on him — not the safest thing to do, considering that McCarver was wired up with all sorts of electronic equipment.

Needless to say, McCarver was furious, but he kept his composure. He contented himself with a sarcastic remark to Sanders as the player walked away. "You're a real man, Deion, a real man."

A WAGA cameraman captured the entire incident on film, including the aftermath, when Sanders went back to the kitchen, filled a pitcher with water and went off in search of *Journal* columnist Moore. That film would later go to the National League office after McCarver filed a complaint. The next day, McCarver said that Sanders had perpetrated "an act of cowardice. . . . It says a lot about him that this sort of thing is his main thrust after his team just won to reach the World Series."

> *"It says a lot about him that this sort of thing is his main thrust after his team just won to reach the World Series."*
>
> CBS ANNOUNCER
> TIM MCCARVER,
> AFTER BEING DOUSED
> WITH WATER BY
> DEION SANDERS

The game inspired some wonderful writing in the papers of the next two days. Some of it was accomplished under incredible deadline pressure. The *Journal-Constitution's* Bradley, for instance, rewrote his entire column in approximately 20 minutes. Here's a sampling, from our paper and others.

Furman Bisher, *Atlanta Journal:*

"How do you say it? How do you write it? It's almost too big, bigger than Bobby Thomson's home run in 1951, bigger than Bill Mazeroski's home run in 1960, bigger than Don Larsen's perfect game, bigger than Stone Mountain. And if you don't think so, just stop any of 51,975 tomahawk wielders — a small clot of Pirates devotees excluded — and they will tell you it's ... it's ... well, THIS BIG!"

Mark Bradley, *Atlanta Journal-Constitution:*

"Of all the miracles worked these past two seasons, from the overhauling of the Dodgers to Otis Nixon's catch, this will forever rank first. Down 2-0 in Game 7 of a series they'd all but blown, three outs from an offseason of second-guessing and finger-pointing, the Atlanta Braves . . . won!"

Steve Hummer, *Journal-Constitution:*

"On the morning after, reconstructing the chain of improbabilities that led from infamy to the World Series, it still seems like building a castle out of gold dust. Nor will it seem any more common one year from now."

Lewis Grizzard, *Journal-Constitution:*

"I don't care. I'm calling Cabrera's hit the greatest moment in Atlanta sports history. I'm calling it one of the greatest moments in the history of the damned game of baseball and don't try to stop me."

Bill Plaschke, *Los Angeles Times:*

"A baseball game was powerful enough to leave the National League's two strongest teams in tears Wednesday night. The Atlanta Braves ended the night hugging and weeping and running around Atlanta-Fulton County Stadium like awestruck children. The Pittsburgh Pirates ended it sobbing into their lockers while wondering if they will ever be able to forget. 'They haven't invented a word to describe this,' said Andy Van Slyke of the Pirates. The Braves would choose 'miracle,' and who could argue."

I went back to the newspaper to get a copy of the home edition. The headline on page A1 was "OH, YES!" On the sports front, it was "Unbelievable!" I finally got home around 4 a.m. Sleep was a ways off.

THURSDAY, OCT. 15

Hullinger called. He told me to come down to WAGA to view the tape of the Sanders-McCarver incident. Later I went out to the stadium; the only Braves there were Glavine and Mazzone. Glavine would start the Series opener against the Toronto Blue Jays, who had beaten Oakland in six games. Mazzone was working with Glavine on his changeup. He would be a different pitcher in the Series, which was now only 24 hours away.

"It's almost too big, bigger than Bobby Thomson's home run in 1951, bigger than Bill Mazeroski's home run in 1960, bigger than Don Larsen's perfect game, bigger than Stone Mountain."

JOURNAL SPORTS EDITOR
FURMAN BISHER

CHAPTER 10

BACK TO THE SERIES

FRIDAY, OCT. 16

AROUND TOWN, THE BIG QUESTION WAS WHETHER THE Braves would drop Sanders from the roster for the Series. He'd only had five at-bats against the Pirates, with no hits and three strikeouts. Plus, he'd thoroughly embarrassed the team with the McCarver incident. But anyone who knew Schuerholz knew he wouldn't do it. The argument for dropping Sanders was adding Peña, but his sore elbow hadn't come around yet. Schuerholz was a bottom-line guy. He'd do whatever he thought would help the Braves win. He'd demonstrated that attitude in the offseason when he'd signed free agent Nixon to a huge contract. He knew he'd get skewered for rewarding a drug abuser, but he also knew the team needed Nixon. "Hey," he told me, "nothing can get in the way of what's best for this team."

In the wake (literally as well as figuratively) of the Sanders-McCarver incident, the *Journal-Constitution's* Sheeley, in his daily "Sportscene" notes column, recalled another incident of a player abusing a reporter during a postgame celebration. That was in 1980, after the Astros won the West title, and outfielder Cesar

Anyone who knew John Schuerholz knew he wouldn't drop Deion Sanders from the World Series roster.

FRANK NIEMEIR

Cedeño pulled *Houston Post* reporter Kenny Hand's ankles out from under him, dragged him a cross a locker-room floor covered with champagne, water and food, and said, "I'm going to teach you how to slide." Sheeley also wrote that there was no truth to the rumor that McCarver was looking for Sanders in the whirlpool so he could toss him a plugged-in hair dryer.

Amid all this mayhem and mirth, the Braves were concerned about Mercker. He had bruised his ribs during the pennant celebration when he jumped on Pendleton and someone else had jumped on him, but doctors couldn't find any fracture. He did some throwing along the sideline during the two off days, and said he felt no discomfort. But Cox held off on a decision. He had until one hour after batting practice began on Saturday to make the call, and he wanted to use all the time available. If Mercker couldn't go, he'd activate Peña or David Nied.

Game 1: Atlanta fans were hoping to run their record to 2-0 in head-to-head competition with the city of Toronto.

Mercker didn't come out onto the field for batting practice, so I asked one of the bat boys to go into the clubhouse and tell him I was looking for him. He came out right away, dressed in shorts and a T-shirt. He was heartbroken. "It's just confusing," he said. "Why go out there and throw two days in a row to prove I'm healthy, and even though I'm healthy, it doesn't matter?"

(Later in the Series, in Toronto, Mercker told me Mazzone had come up to him. "Leo said to me, 'I.J. obviously misquoted you; you better watch out what you say to him.' If he only knew what I really felt."

The sad thing was, Mazzone probably really believed I had put words in Mercker's mouth. To him, if a player thought he was being treated unfairly by Cox, the player could be counted on to react the way military cadets do to a paddling. You know, "Thank you sir, may I have another?"

Cox explained his decision to go with Nied over Peña or Mercker this way: "[Peña] could have gone out there and pitched in the first game and had elbow problems and we would have lost him and not been able to replace him. And we would have been taking a chance with Kent. The biggest thing is, David is healthy."

The *Journal-Constitution* published an 18-page World Series preview section. The front page was to be dominated by a five-point "How the Braves Can Win" graphic, but when I got my paper that morning, I was surprised to discover another element across the top of the front. Someone had decided to treat the Series like the next coming of the Spanish-American War. "Message to Toronto:" read the headline. "This is OUR game!" "OUR" was, of course, in blood-red ink. Who said jingoism was dead? By thunder, no hockey-playing, whale-blubber-eating, Molson-drinking bunch of hose-headed yahoos was going to come sneaking across the border and make off with the championship of the American pastime! In your face, eh!

The Series had a number of interesting subplots. The most obvious, beyond the U.S. vs. Canada angle, was the number of players and coaches who'd spent time with the other team. After his first stint with Atlanta in 1978-81, Cox managed the Blue Jays in '82-85, taking them to their first division championship in his last year there. Williams succeeded him when Cox returned to the Braves, and managed the Jays in '86-89. Toronto's current manager, Cito Gaston, replaced Williams after the club's 12-24 start in '89. Toronto relievers Duane Ward and Mark Eichhorn had pitched for the Braves, and Cabrera had played three games for Toronto in 1989.

Everybody wanted to know how Cox would feel about going back

DAVID TULIS

Game 1: Country singer Billy Ray Cyrus was a hit singing the national anthem.

to Toronto after Game 2, but he said the Blue Jays' new stadium, Sky-Dome, detracted a little bit from the nostalgia. "I wish we were playing in old Exhibition Stadium," he said. "It would bring back a lot of memories."

Another media casualty. Before the game, Justice begged off doing "David's Diary" for WAGA, saying that to remain focused on the series was more important than the $500 a day he was getting from the station. I knew it put Hullinger in an awkward position, but I couldn't fault Justice for his thinking. We're lucky. Olson doesn't have to be focused.

Before the Series could finally start, there was just one more crisis to deal with. It was residue from the NLCS Game 7 celebration on the field. Literally. Seems that when mounted police rode onto the field at the conclusion of the game, a couple of the horses got a little too excited and urinated in the bullpen and near the dugout. It appeared they'd had a lot to drink. The stench was so bad in the bullpen that a four-inch trench had to be dug to let it run off.

At last, the game. Glavine started against Jack Morris, who had beaten the Braves 1-0 in 10 innings in Game 7 of the '91 Series. Morris had left the Twins after that game, signing with the Blue Jays as a free agent. Morris is regarded as one of the toughest competitors in baseball, but Glavine went into this game with an attitude, and it may have helped him come out on top.

Glavine got along well with the media during the season, but come the postseason, he became defensive. As good as he'd been during the '91 and '92 regular seasons (a combined 40-19), he'd been bad in the postseason. He'd been 0-2 in the '91 NLCS, 1-1 in the '91 Series, 0-2 in the '92 NLCS. He felt it was unfair of the media to keep bringing that up. "It's always 'What did you do for me lately?'" he said. Well, that was true. Should we simply have ignored his postseason problems and written that the Braves were a lock to win because Glavine had been so good in the regular season? Of course not. There's a new game every day. "What have you done for me lately?" is a fact of life. The funny thing was, Glavine wasn't reluctant to criticize himself. He just didn't want anybody else doing it.

Glavine's attitude was typical of even the more rational athletes. Under the surface, there was raging paranoia. Us against them. One phrase you always heard ballplayers using when they talked about their accomplishments was "nobody can take that away from us." Every time I heard that, I always wanted to ask, "Who's trying to take it away from you?"

The smart players used this attitude to help motivate themselves. And Glavine was a smart player.

He wasn't necessarily a lucky player, though, and when he gave up a fourth-inning home run to Joe Carter for the game's first run, it appeared his postseason misfortunes might be continuing. He had now allowed four homers in 11 postseason innings after giving up just six in 225 regular-season innings. But in the sixth, with two out and

Photo: DAVID TULIS

DAVID TULIS   DAVID TULIS

two on, Berryhill took Morris deep for a 3-1 lead. It broke a scoreless streak of 18 innings for Atlanta against Morris, but more important, it put the Braves in command of the game.

After giving up the homer to Carter, Glavine had retired the next nine batters, and he continued his mastery the rest of the way, ending up with a four-hitter, walking none and striking out six. This was the Tom Glavine who'd won 19 of his first 22 decisions.

Berryhill, too, was feeling redeemed. "I look at this as an opportunity to show the people that I can play the game," he said.

SUNDAY, OCT. 18

Sanders was back in the news. With Cone starting in Game 2, Cox decided to use Sanders, who hit .600 against the pitcher this season when Cone was with the Mets. The odd man out was left fielder Gant, who was .333 against Cone this season and .281 lifetime, but also was hitless in his last 11 postseason at-bats. The start was only the third one for Sanders since Aug. 31.

Before the game, there arose a controversy that would dwarf anything Sanders had done. A Marine color guard presenting the flags of both countries had the Canadian flag upside down, with the stem of the maple leaf pointing up. The incident was seen by millions of viewers in Canada who were watching the pre-game broadcast. (Ironically, U.S. viewers did not see it, because CBS was showing the finish of "60 Minutes.")

Game 1:
"I look at this as an opportunity to show the people that I can play the game."

DAMON BERRYHILL,
WHO DROVE IN
ALL THREE ATLANTA
RUNS WITH A HOMER

JONATHAN NEWTON

RICH MAHAN

'It was just a human error. They generally don't have a Canadian flag in their color guard. In the excitement, they just attached it wrong."

BRAVES VICE PRESIDENT WAYNE LONG, ON THE GREAT FLAG FLAP

Phones began ringing all over the continent. "We received 200 phone calls within a half-hour, Most of them are outraged and insulted," said Bill Duff, assistant city editor of the Toronto Sun. The Journal-Constitution also received calls from angry Canadians, some of whom — still mad about the "It's OUR Game" headline — refused to believe the paper didn't have something to do with this latest insult.

Uncovering what really had happened wasn't easy. The Braves initially misidentified the color guard as being an Army unit, but it turned out the military men were from the 6th Marine Corps District Headquarters in Atlanta. "It was just a human error," said Braves vice president and director of marketing Wayne Long. "They generally don't have a Canadian flag in their color guard. In the excitement,

184

they just attached it wrong."

The Marines said it was the Braves, not they, who had attached it wrong. Ron Martz, a former *Journal-Constitution* sportswriter who was now the paper's military affairs reporter, spoke to Chief Warrant Officer Randy Gaddo, spokesman for the 6th Marine Corps District. Gaddo would not identify the Marine who carried the flag, but said an unidentified Braves official had attached the flag to the staff. It had to be done quickly, he said, becuse the flag, supplied by the Braves, did not arrive at the stadium until just before the pregame ceremonies. Nobody noticed it was upside down, he said, and it was quickly furled to keep it from flapping in the strong winds. "The first chance they had to see it was when they stepped out on the field, and by then it was too late."

The incident divided Canadians into two groups. One believed the mistake had been made intentionally, as an insult to their country. The other believed it had been an honest mistake, but saw it as an example of ignorance and insensitivity toward their country by Americans.

Resurrected in all this were the hard feelings of many in Toronto about their city being beaten out by Atlanta for the 1996 Summer Olympics. How are those rubes going to get all the flags of the other nations at the Olympics right, they wanted to know, if they can't even figure out which end of a maple leaf is up?

Major League Baseball issued an apology, and Gen. Carl E. Mundy Jr., the Marine Corps commandant and a native of Atlanta, personally apologized to Derek Burney, Canada's ambassador to the U.S., but the damage had been done. It was war.

Once the flags had been put away and the game started, Sanders didn't waste any time making Cox's decision to play him look good. Batting second behind Nixon, he ripped Cone's first pitch deep to right, where right fielder Dave Winfield caught it with his back against the wall.

The Braves broke out on top in the second inning, Justice scoring on a wild pitch. The Blue Jays almost tied it in the fourth, when a Smoltz pitch in the dirt got away from Berryhill. With Roberto Alomar barreling in from third, Berryhill retrieved the ball and hurriedly flipped it to Smoltz covering the plate. Alomar slid headfirst as Smoltz slapped down the tag. Out, signaled plate umpire Mike Reilly. Replays, however, indicated it was a bad call.

The Braves added another run in the bottom of the fourth when Lemke singled Bream home, but Toronto tied it with a two-out rally in the top of the fifth, Cone singling home Pat Borders and Devon White singling home Manny Lee. The Braves came back with two runs of their own in the fifth, Justice singling home Sanders and Hunter scoring Pendleton with a sacrifice fly.

With a 4-2 lead going into the eighth, the Braves had to feel good behind Smoltz, who had been named the MVP of the playoffs. This was starting to look like the first two games of the playoffs. But the whole complexion of the Series was about to change.

Game 2: The flag incident divided Canadians into two groups. One believed it was an intentional insult to their country. The other believed it was an honest mistake, but saw it as an example of insensitivity toward their country.

JONATHAN NEWTON

Game 2: Damon Berryhill retrieved the ball and flipped it to John Smoltz. Roberto Alomar slid headfirst as Smoltz slapped down the tag. Out, signaled plate umpire Mike Reilly. Replays indicated it was a bad call.

DAVID TULIS

Smoltz got White on a fly ball to center to lead off the eighth, but then gave up a double down the left-field line to Roberto Alomar, the second baseman some thought was the best at his position in baseball. Carter singled to center, putting runners at the corners, and Winfield singled to right, scoring Alomar and sending Carter to third, where he represented the tying run. Three straight hits, and Cox had seen enough. He called on Stanton, wanting a lefty-lefty matchup against John Olerud, and Stanton got Olerud to pop to Pendleton. He then brought on Reardon to face right-handed hitting Kelly Gruber, and Reardon struck him out. Crisis averted.

In the ninth, however, Reardon walked pinch hitter Derek Bell with one out. With reliever Duane Ward, the former Brave, due to hit next, Gaston called on Ed Sprague to pinch hit. Sprague, a backup catcher, had played in only 22 games during the regular season. He was best known for his family connections; his father, Ed Sr., pitched in the majors from 1968-76, and his wife, Kristen, had won a gold medal for synchronized swimming for the United States in the Barcelona Olympics.

Little-used backup catcher. Clutch situation. The omens were bad. For Reardon's first pitch, Berryhill called for a fastball, low and out-side. It was low, but over the plate. Thanks to teammate Rance Mulliniks, Sprague was expecting it. "Rance told me to look for a

Game 2: Deion Sanders put the Braves ahead in the fifth, scoring on a single by David Justice.

*Game 2:
As Ed Sprague's
home run off
Jeff Reardon sailed
over the fence,
Deion Sanders
could only watch.*

DAVID TULIS

Facing page: FRANK NIEMEIR

ENCORE!

JONATHAN NEWTON

fastball low," Sprague said. When it came, Sprague deposited it into the left-field seats as Sanders watched helplessly.

"It's pretty tough for this to happen to me in a World Series game," said Reardon. "All I can do is go out and try to get them tomorrow."

Well, Tuesday, actually. Monday would be devoted to traveling to Toronto for the first World Series game ever played in Canada. I couldn't wait to see what kind of reception we Ugly Americans would get at the border.

Game 2: Jays third baseman Kelly Gruber mocked the chop as he left the field.

MONDAY, OCT. 19

A day for flag flap fallout. Some Canadians, including Jim Elliott, Canada's Consul General, were willing to forgive and forget. "It was an unfortunate incident that obviously nobody planned to have happen," he said, "and it's better buried and forgotten." The Canadian press, however, especially the super-competitive media in Toronto, which has three daily newspapers, was unrelenting in seeking comment from official Atlanta. In Atlanta Mayor Maynard Jackson's office, which had been besieged by calls from Canadian reporters, press secretary Deb Speights said, "Clearly it was an error on someone's part, but the city was not involved in coordinating the World Series or that opening." The Atlanta Committee for the Olympic Games was irritated at the guilt-by-association suggestions that they wouldn't be able to handle proper flag etiquette when the Summer Games came to Atlanta in 1996. "ACOG didn't fly the Canadian flag upside down," huffed spokesman Bob Brennan. "Anyway, we have a protocol office that pays attention to those kinds of details. We've been flying the flags of all the Olympic nations at a number of events for a while, and we haven't had any complaints."

But leave it to Blauser to get in the best comment. Referring to the unfortunate Marine who carried the upside-down flag, he said, "I bet that guy is still doing pushups."

For the trip to Toronto, I decided to take the Braves' charter.

There were a couple of advantages to this. If anyone had anything newsworthy to say on the trip, I'd get it firsthand. (This was rarely the case, but it occasionally happened.) When we landed, we'd get through customs faster. And I'd be flying in an L-1011. That was no small factor, considering that the travel plans for the rest of our reporters and photographers included changing planes in Syracuse and taking a Beechcraft 1900 puddle-jumper from Syracuse to Toronto. One of our people later told me the plane had only nine rows of seats (a "row" consisted of one seat on each side of the aisle), was so small you couldn't stand up, and had no stewardess, just a tape recording of one giving safety instructions. Said Terry Moore, after wedging himself into his seat, "Normally I have a rule against flying in anything smaller than my living room."

Yes, the charter was definitely the way to go. More than 200 players, coaches, front-office personnel and spouses were aboard, and many of them slept through most of the flight. (Try that in a Beechcraft 1900.) After being hustled through customs, we boarded the bus for the hotel, the Hilton in downtown Toronto. It was chilly, but the cold air felt good. As Lake Ontario appeared on our right, we could see SkyDome and its neighbor, the CN Tower. Even in a city renowned for its modern architecture, they were an impressive sight. And yes, it's called SkyDome, not the SkyDome. Canadians, for reasons that have never been clear to me, seem to have an aversion to definite articles.

The Braves didn't seem to be bothered by the Game 2 loss. "I think we would all rather have it the easy way," said Pendleton. "But I guess fate has put it where we always have to play with our backs to the wall. To a lot of people, things didn't come easy, and I think that's true with the Atlanta Braves. Before I got here, this team was struggling to just win. And now that we've found a way to win, we're struggling to do it where we can be comfortable and enjoy it."

They also weren't concerned about playing in SkyDome, even though they'd lost all four World Series games they'd played last year in Minneapolis's Metrodome. But the Metrodome was unique. It had a light-colored roof, which made it tough to pick up fly balls, and its acoustics made it the loudest place I'd ever been in. "The Skydome is a real dome, a baseball dome," said Smoltz, ignoring Canadian speech patterns. "I don't know what they play in the Metrodome, but it's not baseball."

Sanders, meanwhile, had found a media outlet to vent his frustrations. He was upset that the Braves had criticized him for playing for the Falcons while the playoff series against Pittsburgh was still going on, but he still didn't want to talk to the Atlanta media. So he went to a reporter from New York Newsday and ripped Schuerholz.

"They used the press against me," he said. "I wasn't talking to the press then because I don't get along with them down here [in Atlanta]. Why did he [Schuerholz] go to the media? Because he knew I wouldn't retaliate." Sanders said he wasn't going to worry about

> *"Fate has put it where we always have to play with our backs to the wall. To a lot of people, things didn't come easy, and I think that's true with the Atlanta Braves."*
>
> TERRY PENDLETON, ON THE BRAVES' REACTION TO LOSING GAME 2

Game 3:
In the ninth inning,
Bobby Cox became the
first manager since
1985 to be ejected from
a Series game.
He threw a helmet
onto the field after
Jeff Blauser was called
out on a check swing.

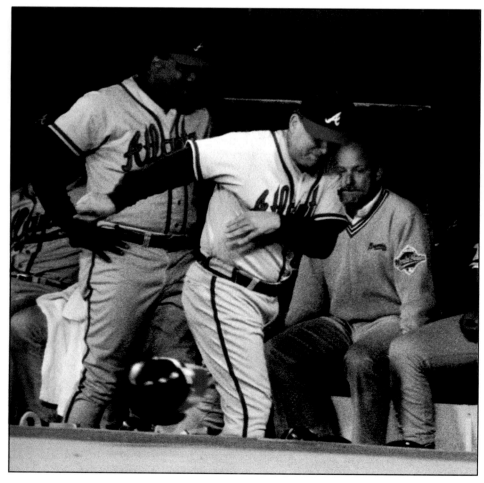

DAVID TULIS

ENCORE!

nearly became the victim of the first World Series triple play in 72 years. Only a blown call by second-base umpire Bob Davidson saved them from that distinction. Sanders and Pendleton led off with singles, putting runners at first and second. Justice then drilled a ball deep to center field. White, sprinting away from the plate, made a great catch just before crashing into the wall. He then fired the ball back to second baseman Alomar, who relayed to Olerud at first before Pendleton could get back to the bag. Olerud then spotted Sanders caught between second and third, and fired to third baseman Gruber. Gruber chased Sanders back toward second, diving for Sanders's feet as Sanders dove for the base. Davidson called Sanders safe, although replays later indicated he should have been out.

Later, the scoring on the play was changed. Pendleton had actually passed Sanders at second, and was called out for that.

The Braves had a 2-1 lead going into the bottom of the eighth, thanks to single runs scored by Sanders and Nixon, but Avery surrendered a game-tying home run to Gruber, the third baseman's first hit in the postseason.

In the ninth, Cox became the first manager since 1985 to be ejected from a Series game. He threw a helmet onto the field after Blauser was called out on a check swing and Hunter was thrown out trying to steal second on the play. In violation of baseball rules, Cox remained in the tunnel and managed from there, but it hardly made any difference.

DAVID TULIS

*Game 3:
Joe Carter's
fourth-inning
home run gave
the Jays a 1-0 lead.*

WEDNESDAY, OCT. 21

The Braves trailed by only two games to one, but their confidence appeared shot. There was little life during batting practice before Game 4, and several players told me the clubhouse was like a morgue. There was some startling news: Davidson had admitted he "probably" blew the call on the triple play. "When I first called the play, I thought I was 100 percent right," he said. "It was right there. It was right in front of me. Then I saw the replays and the pictures, and I thought I probably missed the play. No one feels worse than I do."

DAVID TULIS

Well, maybe Reardon. He told me that usually, no matter how bad he was pitching, his wife Phebe could always console him, but even she was upset about the current state of affairs. "This is the worst thing that has ever happened in my career," he said.

You couldn't help but feel sorry for Reardon. You also couldn't help but feel that what really was bothering him was the growing realization that he had grown old and lost the stuff that made him one of the best closers of all time.

The Braves again lost by a run, this time failing to produce against Jimmy Key, who was making his first start of the postseason. With the 2-1 loss, they now faced a 3-1 deficit. In Series history, 34 teams had won Game 4 to take a 3-1 lead. Only six had then lost the Series.

The loser was Glavine, but this time he was heroic in defeat. He gave up a solo home run to Borders in the third and another run in the seventh on a two-out hit by White.

The Braves had a chance to tie it in the eighth. Gant led off with a

ENCORE!

Game 4:
Tom Glavine lost, but
he was heroic in defeat.
He gave up a solo
home run to Pat
Borders in the third
and another run
in the seventh.

DAVID TULIS

double down the left-field line, his first hit in 17 at-bats. Hunter tried to bunt him to third, and did it so well he reached base himself, too. First and third, nobody out. Berryhill up. Cox put on the steal sign for Hunter. But Berryhill, on his own, tried to bunt. Disaster. He popped the ball up, and Borders quickly grabbed it. "I don't know what he was thinking," an angry Cox said later.

"If I put down a halfway decent bunt, Ronnie scores and I've got a chance to reach," said Berryhill. "I've attempted it a few times, but never popped it up. That's the worst thing that could have happened . . . then I wouldn't have to answer these questions."

Still, there was only one out. Lemke smashed a ball up the middle that for a split second looked as if it would score Gant and get Hunter to second. But no. The ball hit the front slope of the mound and deflected toward third base. Gruber alertly barehanded the ball and threw Lemke out. Now there were two out, Hunter on second, and a run in. Gaston called for Ward, the righthander. Nixon, batting left-handed, struck out swinging at a pitch in the dirt, but reached first

198

FRANK NIEMEIR

when the ball got past Borders for a wild pitch. Hunter took third. Blauser, a right-handed hitter who had just one hit in his last 10 at-bats, was due up. Cox had two lefthanders — Bream and Sanders, the only two Braves who were hitting over .300 in the Series — available on the bench, but he let Blauser hit. Cox said he never considered a pinch hitter.

On the first pitch, Nixon stole second. Almost any type of hit now would score both the tying and go-ahead runs. Blauser smashed the ball down the first-base line, but Olerud was there. He went to one knee and stopped it, then stepped on first for the final out. Tom Henke retired the side in the ninth, and the Braves were on the brink of elimination.

Their attitude didn't inspire optimism, either. Nixon told me after the game that there were a lot of ongoing problems with the team. Said Glavine, "There were three or four times when I came in there [to the dugout] and started hollering just to break the tension."

Now it was up to Smoltz. Again.

*Game 4:
Kelly Gruber was
in a daze after sliding
hard to score the
Blue Jays' second run.*

Got a call around noon from the office. Somebody had heard Justice on his regular radio report on Star 94 criticizing his teammates for lack of enthusiasm in the dugout. Our TV/radio reporter, Prentis Rogers, was going to get the transcript from the station, but the office read me some of his remarks. I was to start calling other players to get their reaction.

My first calls were to Nixon and Blauser. Neither answered in his hotel room, so I left messages. Both called back within a few minutes.

Part of what Justice said was, "Our bench was dead. It looked like guys just showed up for the game, a spring training game. The mood from the beginning of the game seemed like the guys were not totally into it. The way it appeared was the enthusiasm was never there."

Blauser's reaction was predictable. "Look who's saying it," he said. Blauser didn't have much use for Justice.

Nixon surprised me with his anger. He was furious with Justice. He said he hadn't talked to him in a long time. Then he told me about an incident that happened during the locker-room celebration after the pennant-winning Game 7 victory over the Pirates. Sanders, in the course of throwing water at everyone he could find, tried to douse Justice. He missed, however, and instead soaked Justice's fiancee, actress Halle Berry. Justice was furious. Nixon said the two almost came to blows. Nixon wasn't a fan of Berry. He said she had worn a hat and sunglasses on the charter to Toronto, trying to be incognito. I guess it had worked; I hadn't noticed her. "She does a couple of movies," he said, "and suddenly she thinks she's Janet Jackson. Her head is as big as Toronto." Nixon advised me to watch the outfielders when Cox was changing pitchers. The center fielder and left fielder would come together to talk, but Justice would never join in.

Those were the only two players I could reach by phone. I went to the park early to talk to the others. Nobody wanted to touch the Justice issue. And Cox, who was the person I most needed to talk to, was staying in the clubhouse, where he knew reporters couldn't get to him. It was getting close to the time when the media would be required to leave the field. But I lucked out. Jim Small of the major-league publicity office told me Cox was in the tunnel that connected the dugout and the clubhouse. I could go in there. I ran in and asked him about Justice, quickly reading him the transcript. He went crazy, cursing and stamping his feet. "It's a crock of crap," he said, more or less, "a bunch of bull. We were never more fired up. In my estimation, these guys do these things, and they don't know what they're saying."

Cox went back into the clubhouse to confront Justice. Nixon later told me that Justice blamed everything on me, but Nixon got up and defended my position, asking, "Who has the FM radio show?" In the few minutes he had before the game started, Cox knew he had to refocus the team's attention on the game, and get it off Justice. Ironically, the first part of it was essentially the same point Justice had been trying to make.

> *"It's a bunch of bull. We were never more fired up. In my estimation, these guys do these things, and they don't know what they're saying."*
>
> BOBBY COX, AFTER HEARING REPORTS THAT DAVID JUSTICE HAD QUESTIONED HIS TEAMMATES' ENTHUSIASM IN GAME 4

While all this was going on, Bream was in the interview room saying the same things about his teammates that Justice had, but without drawing fire to himself. "I truly believe there are two different ways of going out on the ballfield," Bream said. "You can get excited about playing, but you also have to have the right kind of mindset, the right kind of focus. I think that's where we're lacking."

So why didn't Cox blast Bream as he had Justice? Timing, mostly. He wasn't aware of Bream's comments. Bream had been in the interview room while the other players were on the field and Cox was in the clubhouse. By the time Bream's remarks had been transcribed and circulated in the press box, it was too late to talk to Cox or the players. And once the game was over, there were other concerns to address.

Cox wasn't the only one staying in the clubhouse. Gant wasn't in the starting lineup for the third time in the Series, and he didn't come out for batting practice. When I asked batting coach Clarence Jones about this, he became very defensive, saying Gant's knee was bothering him. Then Cox told me Gant had the flu. But another reporter overheard Cox saying to Jones, "Hey, what's the deal with Gant. Is he sick?" Gant wasn't sick. He was upset and embarrassed.

With all this as a prelude to the game, the Braves might have been expected to disintegrate. But they demonstrated a remarkable ability to put the dissension behind them, right from the start. They scored in the first and fourth innings, let the Blue Jays tie it twice, then went ahead for good on a Lonnie Smith grand slam in the fifth. Smoltz, with three innings of relief from Stanton, shut down the Blue Jays the rest of the way, and the Series was headed back to Atlanta. If they could just win both remaining games at Atlanta-Fulton County Stadium, the Braves would be world champs.

Nixon started things off immediately with a double down the left-field line. Sanders struck out, but Nixon stole third. Pendleton then doubled down the right-field line to score Nixon. It appeared for a moment as if it would be a big inning, but Justice struck out and Smith flied to right.

The Blue Jays tied it in the bottom of the second when Borders scored Olerud from second with a double down the left-field line.

The Braves went ahead 2-1 in the fourth on a home run by Justice. His focus certainly seemed to be all right. The Blue Jays came back in the bottom of the inning when Borders again drove Olerud home from second, this time with a single. Borders was getting slaughtered by the Braves' base-stealers, but he was having his revenge at the plate.

The fifth inning was the turning point. It all happened with two out. Berryhill struck out leading off, and Lemke grounded to second. But Nixon singled, stole second and came home on another single by Sanders. Sanders was another one who didn't seem to be letting the controversy swirling around him affect his play. He was the club's leading hitter by a wide margin. Pendleton hit another double down

Game 5: Ron Gant wasn't in the starting lineup for the third time in the Series, and he didn't come out for batting practice. He was upset and embarrassed.

FRANK NIEMEIR

Opposite page: W. A. BRIDGES JR.

Game 5:
"I saw Joe Carter looking up and I started screaming, 'Get out of here! Get out of here!'"

LONNIE SMITH,
DESCRIBING HIS GRAND
SLAM OFF JACK MORRIS

the right-field line, sending Sanders to third, and Justice was intentionally walked to load the bases. Up came Lonnie Smith. He was in the lineup as the designated hitter, which is used in the Series only in the games played in the American League park. Gaston had David Wells warming up in the bullpen, but decided to stick with Morris. The count went to 1-and-2. Morris tried to power a high fastball past Smith. At 37, Morris was seven months and six days older than Smith. Neither had the physical skills he once did, but both were proud, fierce competitors. Both believed in pitting strength against strength, and may the better man win.

Smith swung. A little late, but not too much. The ball took off toward right field in a high arc. "I felt I hit it well enough to at least hit the wall," he said. "Then I saw Joe Carter looking up and I started screaming, 'Get out of here! Get out of here!'"

It did. Carter could only watch. And listen. There they were, the boos, welling up from the stands. For Smith? No. For Morris? Only partially. For Gaston? Bingo. Even in this remarkable season, when he had brought his team one game from the ultimate championship, Gaston still was taking a lot of grief from the Toronto fans. They felt he'd left Morris in too long. It was a pretty easy conclusion to reach.

"I guess the results show that perhaps I did," Gaston said. "I believe in Jack a lot. Without Jack, we wouldn't be here. I gave him a chance to get out of that inning. It just didn't work out. I feel bad for him."

Smoltz lasted two more innings. Cox lifted him for Stanton after he walked Lee leading off the seventh. Cox wasn't going to take any chances. "He was pitching real good only in spurts," Cox said. "He told me [before the seventh] that he had one more inning left."

"Even though I had a lot of adrenaline early in the game," said Smoltz, "I completely lost it as the game went on."

The big question after the game was whether Smith would talk to the media. When he had hit home runs in three consecutive games in the '91 Series, he had maintained silence. Jim Schultz, the Braves' public relations director, expected him to do it again. But there he was, talking freely this time.

The first question was obvious. Did the grand slam make him feel he'd redeemed himself for the crucial base-running mistake he'd made in the final game of the '91 Series?

"Not really," he said. "I've been criticized my whole career. I've been criticized by our own hometown reporters because I'm a black man. For another, I've been considered a mediocre ballplayer my whole career."

Both these charges were patently ridiculous. The race issue didn't even deserve comment. As far as the mediocre ballplayer charge, well, Smith had it over .300 six times. He was a career .291 hitter for the regular season, and .290 for four previous World Series. He'd beaten drugs. He'd been the comeback player of the year in 1989. He'd been runner-up to Atlanta's Dale Murphy in the 1982 NL MVP voting. He

Game 5: Booing Toronto fans felt Jack Morris had been left in too long. It was a pretty easy conclusion to reach.

DAVID TULIS

had three World Series championship rings. Yes, he'd lost some speed, he was a mediocre fielder at best (his nickname in the media was "Skates," for the unsteady way he ran after fly balls), and he'd made an egregious base-running mistake at the worst possible time of the '91 Series, a blunder that probably cost the Braves the title. Smith and the media were simply at an impasse. He'd always feel the reporters and columnists had treated him like dirt. And they'd always feel he'd done the same thing to them.

I had only an hour to finish my game story because I wanted to catch the team charter back to Atlanta. I wondered if there'd be any more reaction to the Justice situation. There wasn't. The plane was strangely quiet, virtually the only sound coming from the movie, "A League of Their Own," about a wartime baseball league for women. When we landed at Hartsfield, almost 5,000 fans were there to greet the team. It was 4 a.m. "Hey," yelled Skip Caray when he saw them, "get a life, people." When the bus pulled into the stadium after the drive from the airport, there were another 1,000 or so fans. When do these people sleep?

There was no workout scheduled for Friday. The players needed some time away from each other.

FRIDAY, OCT. 23

Everybody knew what the Braves had to do in Game 6. I decided there was no point in calling Cox at home. Let the guy have some peace for a day. What was he going to say, anyway? It was the consensus in the press box that Cox was feeling the pressure of being on the verge of losing consecutive World Series, and his club was reflecting his tension. He'd been down this road before. His Blue Jays club had lost the '85 playoffs to Kansas City after being up 3-1.

I went out to the park to watch the Blue Jays work out. They appeared to be very relaxed. Why shouldn't they be? With no Braves players to be interviewed, Schultz asked Schuerholz if he'd talk. Immediately, he was besieged with questions about the dissension on the team. He tried to downplay the situation. On my radio spot, I was asked who would win the Series. For the first time, I really felt the Braves' magic had run out. I didn't think they could beat both Cone and Guzman back-to-back. Come Saturday, I'd get at least the first part of the answer.

When we landed at Hartsfield, almost 5,000 fans were there to greet the team. It was 4 a.m.

CHAPTER 11

MIRACLES FALL SHORT

SATURDAY, OCT. 24

I DECIDED TO GET TO THE PARK EARLIER THAN USUAL. I had been arriving four hours before gametime, but now I wanted to talk to a certain player before he went into the locker room, so I got there at 3:30, five hours before the first pitch was to be thrown.

I wanted to know what the reaction in the locker room was to my article on the turmoil. The player agreed to tell me, but only on condition I never identify him. He said that during the team meeting held before Game 6, Justice had stood up and said I was trying to stir up problems and the club should shut me off. I already knew, of course, that Nixon had defended me. This wasn't the first time that Justice had tried to get his teammates to stop talking to me. He'd been somewhat successful after their 5-1 loss to Pittsburgh in Game 1 of the 1991 playoffs, when I'd written that the Braves had looked as if they had stage fright. The Braves were offended, and Justice was able to get most of his teammates to ignore me.

This wasn't the first time that Justice had tried to get his teammates to stop talking to me.

LOUIE FAVORITE

This time was different, though. Many of the players had come up to me and told me what Justice was trying to do. They weren't going along with it this time.

Before the game, the Braves decided to play some head games with the Blue Jays. During the Braves' batting practice at SkyDome, the Blue Jays had played soft, relaxing music. So assistant publicist Glen Serra, with permission from Schuerholz, retaliated. As the Jays were taking batting practice at Atlanta-Fulton County Stadium, he had stadium music operator John Ioannides play selections ranging from Carly Simon's "Itsy Bitsy Spider" to Placido Domingo singing "O Sole Mio" and "Somewhere My Love."

"We just thought our fans could use a little change of pace," deadpanned Schuerholz. "It's not entirely unintentional, though."

Carter summed up the Blue Jays' reaction very nicely when he looked up into the stands and observed to no one in particular, "Nice bleeping music."

Finally, game time. Avery vs. Cone. The Blue Jays broke on top in the first when White led off with a single, stole second, went to third on a groundout by Alomar and scored on a sacrifice fly by Carter. The Braves came back to tie it in the third when Sanders hit a one-out double, stole third and scored on a sacrifice fly by Pendleton.

In the CBS booth, McCarver said about Sanders, "If the Braves

Game 6:
Finally, game time.
Steve Avery vs.
David Cone.
Atlanta fans vs.
Toronto's Coneheads.
Both pitchers
were gone by
the seventh inning.

win, he'd have to be considered for the MVP."

But in the fourth, the Jays went back on top 2-1 on a leadoff homer by Maldonado. It stayed that way until the Braves came to bat in the bottom of the ninth. It looked like this would be their last hurrah.

Avery and Cone were both long gone. Cox pulled Avery after the fourth, calling on first Pete Smith, then Stanton, then Wohlers. Cone departed after six innings, giving way to first Todd Stottlemyre, then Wells, then Ward. Now the Jays' closer, Tom Henke, was on to nail down the championship.

Blauser led off with a single, and the crowd began stirring. Berry-hill sacrificed him to second. Cox sent Lonnie Smith up to hit for Lemke, and he walked. Wohlers was due up next, but Cox called on Cabrera. Could lightning strike twice?

"He's going to do it again," I found myself thinking. "They won't have to worry about tearing this stadium down in 1996. He's going to get a hit, the Braves will win tomorrow and these people will do it themselves for free."

Henke was being careful, and ran the count to 2-2. After three straight foul balls, Cabrera lined a shot to left field. Another miracle? Maldonado, thinking the ball would sink, ran in, then realized in horror that it was over his head. Desperately, he leaped. The ball whacked into his glove. Two out.

The whole season was in Nixon's hands. "I just knew I was going to get the runner in," he said. "It's that feeling you get when you walk up to the plate sometimes." Feeling or no feeling, however, he quickly fell into an 0-and-2 hole. But then he slapped a single to left, and Blauser rounded third and headed for home. Some say a good throw would have had him, but this wasn't a good throw. It sailed far over Borders's head, all the way to the screen. Blauser scored, Smith took third and Nixon went to second. Unbelievable. Suddenly the Braves had the winning run standing on third base. One more hit and they'd force a seventh game, and who could bet against a club so well-versed in the ways of miracles?

Sanders would have been next up, a left-handed batter against the right-handed Henke, but Cox had pinch-hit for him with Gant in the seventh, with two out, Nixon on first and the left-handed Wells in the game. Nixon had been caught stealing, so this would be Gant's first at-bat. Gaston had the righty-righty matchup he wanted. Henke got Gant to fly to center, and the teams headed into extra innings.

The 10th inning passed uneventfully. Leibrandt was now pitching for the Braves, and he gave up only a one-out single by Gruber. Henke retired Pendleton on a grounder to first, then gave way to Key, who got Justice on a grounder to second and Bream on one to first.

Then came the 11th.

Gaston wasn't going to hit for his pitcher unless he had a scoring opportunity, so he let Key lead off. He fouled to Bream at first. But with White crowding the plate, Leibrandt hit him with a pitch. "I was

Game 6:
Fans had a tough time finding tickets. Some watched the game on a big-screen TV in a nearby parking lot. Others searched for tickets, some more desperately than others.

210

RICH ADDICKS

JONATHAN NEWTON

JONATHAN NEWTON

Game 6:
"I just knew I was going to get the runner in," he said. *"It's that feeling you get when you walk up to the plate sometimes."*

OTIS NIXON,
ON HIS NINTH-INNING
HIT THAT DROVE IN
THE TYING RUN

FRANK NIEMEIR

212

ENCORE!

DAVID TULIS

trying to come inside," said Leibrandt. "I wasn't trying to throw a ball. I was trying to get him out. He didn't move a heck of a lot. A couple of inches the other way and it's a strike. The ball wasn't that much inside."

Alomar then singled to center. White stopped at second. The next two batters were both righthanders, Carter and Winfield, and Cox had three righthanders in his bullpen in Reardon, Freeman and Nied. Reardon, in fact, had been warming up. But Cox stuck with the left-handed Leibrandt, saying later, "He gets right-handers out." A year before, same game, same inning, Cox had let Leibrandt pitch to right-handed Kirby Puckett of the Twins. Puckett had led the majors with a .406 average against lefthanders during the season, but Cox felt it was more significant that he had fanned Puckett twice in Game 1.

So here we were again. Leibrandt and Cox both on the spot. This time, however, Cox got away with it, as Leibrandt induced Carter to hit a lazy fly ball to center for the second out. But their luck ran out with Winfield, who at 41 was the oldest player on either team. Eleven

Game 6: "He gets right-handers out."

BOBBY COX, EXPLAINING WHY HE LEFT IN LEFTHANDER CHARLIE LEIBRANDT TO FACE JOE CARTER AND DAVE WINFIELD

DAVID TULIS

Game 6:
"I know he's looking for it. He knows it's coming."

CHARLIE LEIBRANDT,
EXPLAINING THE PITCH
DAVE WINFIELD HIT FOR
A DOUBLE TO DRIVE IN

years before, when Winfield played for the New York Yankees, he'd endured a miserable postseason that included a .154 average in the American League playoffs and an .045 mark in the World Series. Yankees owner George Steinbrenner had sarcastically dubbed him "Mr. May" in mocking contrast to Reggie Jackson's "Mr. October." The insult had stung Winfield, but he'd never been on another team that had made it to the postseason, so he'd never had an opportunity to redeem himself.

Until now.

Leibrandt threw Winfield a changeup, his signature pitch. The same one he'd thrown to Puckett. It also had the same flaw. It was over the plate, something Leibrandt never meant to do.

"I know he's looking for it. He knows it's coming," said Leibrandt. It was just a matter of executing. It was too good a pitch.

"He gave me a pitch I could whack," said Winfield. And that's just what he did, down the third-base line and into the left-field corner. White scored. Alomar scored. It was 4-2. Maldonado popped out to Belliard at second, and the Braves girded for yet another comeback.

Previous page: DAVID TULIS

Game 6:
"I just didn't get it down where I wanted to. After the first pitch, I thought it would be the perfect opportunity for me to get it down. If I get it down, it's a game. I didn't, so it's over."

OTIS NIXON, EXPLAINING WHY HE TRIED TO BUNT FOR A BASE HIT WITH TWO OUT AND THE TYING RUN ON THIRD

RICH MAHAN

DAVID TULIS

Game 6:
The game, the Series
and the season were
over. Major League
Baseball had its first
non–American
champion.

For those into omens, they weren't bad. The batting order was the same as it had been in the ninth, and again, Blauser led off with a single. Berryhill hit what appeared to be a double-play ball to shortstop Alfredo Griffin, but Griffin, who had come on after Lee was lifted for a pinch hitter in the 10th, booted it, and Blauser made it all the way to third. Smoltz came on to run for Berryhill, and Belliard sacrificed him to second. Blauser held at third. Once again, a hit could bring home two runs and tie the score. And they had an out to play with.

Leibrandt was due up, but he was done. Hunter was called to pinch hit. He grounded to first, but Blauser scored and Smoltz went to third. They needed one more run to stay alive.

Gaston brought on Mike Timlin, a righthander, to face the switch-hitting Nixon. Batting from the left side put Nixon two steps closer to first base, and he tried to take advantage by dragging a bunt down the first-base line. But Timlin was ready. Carter had told him to be alert for the possibility before Nixon came up. So when Nixon laid the ball down, a little too hard and a little too close to the mound, Timlin pounced on it and threw to Carter. The game, the Series and the season were over. Major League Baseball had its first non-American champion. The Braves had their second straight October hangover.

"I just didn't get it down where I wanted to," said Nixon. "After

218

DAVID TULIS

RICH MAHAN

*The Braves —
and their fans —
had their second
straight October
hangover.*

JOHNNY CRAWFORD

Previous page: RICH MAHAN

FRANK NIEMEIR

the first pitch I thought it would be the perfect opportunity for me to get it down. If I get it down, it's a game. I didn't, so it's over."

Cox refused to question Nixon's decision. "I don't blame him one bit for that," he said.

In the clubhouse afterward, Pendleton asked all the reporters to leave for a few minutes so he could address the club. Later, he tried to explain his feelings about losing two years in a row.

"It's basically the same [feeling as last year]," he said. "We didn't win, and that's the bottom line. This winter is going to be a gut check for us. I know the fans appreciated what we accomplished. We're in some pain, some real pain."

Inside the stadium, many in the sellout crowd remained standing after the final out, chanting "Braves, Braves, Braves" in tribute to their heroes.

At SkyDome more than 45,000 fans watched the game on the Jumbotron TV screen. When the last out was made they spilled onto the field, dancing and cheering. Flags were long forgotten.

Said Winfield, "This is the most fun I've ever had playing professional baseball. I'll tell you, I'm the oldest guy in the room, but I'm also the happiest."

Borders, who hit safely in all six Series games for a .450 average, was named MVP.

It was now over, some 217 days of baseball. But I had no time for reflecting. I had exactly 30 minutes to pound out one last game story.

"In the end," I wrote, "there were no tears. No emotion. No sound."

ENCORE!

FRANK NIEMEIR

*The "Grand Slam Salute to the Braves"
wasn't anything like last year, when an
estimated 750,000 lined the streets for a parade,
but this was safer and saner. A crowd of about
26,000 showed up, as did most of the Braves.*

THE 1992 ATLANTA BRAVES

The last 60 or so hours had been filled with "what ifs" and "whys." Some people actually called our paper and asked, "Why did Nixon bunt?" Others wanted to know why did Cox do this, why did Cox do that? The answer, once and for all, to all such questions: Because they thought it would work.

I went over to the stadium for the "Grand Slam Salute to the Braves" that had been planned by the city and Fulton County. It wasn't anything like last year, when an estimated 750,000 lined the streets for a parade, but this was safer and saner. A crowd of about 26,000 showed up, as did most of the Braves. Missing were Reardon, Belliard, Berryhill, Bream, Nied, Lopez and Sanders. Sanders was across town filming a Nike commercial.

I went down to the clubhouse and said my goodbyes. Cox had already left, but most everyone else was there. A few players hugged each other.

As I walked out of the clubhouse for the final time this year, I couldn't help thinking that it wasn't yet over for me. There were still postseason awards, offseason operations and ticket-price increases to write about. The possible pursuit of Bonds, now a free agent, had to be kept up with. And the expansion draft was less than a month away.

Out in the parking lot, a few fans were still hanging around, hoping to get another peek at their favorite player. As I pulled out of the lot, I noticed a little boy holding a sign that read: "We'll get 'em next year."

All I could think of was that in 115 days, it would all start again.

AFTERWORD

'WE JUST HAVEN'T WON THE BIG ONE'

BY GREG OLSON

THE TEAM'S GOAL WAS AN OBVIOUS ONE, TO GET TO THE World Series and win it. When the season started, we certainly weren't playing good baseball. When we were getting good pitching, we were scoring one or two runs. When we were getting five or six runs, our pitchers weren't going five innings. We just couldn't get it together.

I can't remember the exact date, but we were ahead of St. Louis by nine runs and we got beat. That was early May (May 9), and we didn't bounce right back, but I know that woke me up, and a few others.

The lucky thing was, the rest of the division wasn't doing anything. Then all of a sudden, it changed. It was the pitching. And we started getting the clutch two-out hits. Then came the steamroll mode, winning every series no matter where we were playing. I knew by the All-Star break it was going to be a two-team race with Cincinnati. And there is no question we benefited from their injuries. The Reds had trouble with their position players, and they had to start some hodgepodge players at times. None of our guys really went down.

Greg Olson: I knew by the All-Star break it was going to be a two-team race with Cincinnati.

When I got hurt I think there were 18 games left, and it was really over. It seemed like Cincinnati was pretty much defeated. But I'll never forget getting hit by Ken Caminiti at the plate. I felt this hot feeling in my leg. Bubba [assistant trainer Jeff Porter] came out and cut off my shoe and took my pants and sock down. I looked at him and said, "Tell me it's just a badly sprained ankle." But I could tell by his glassy eyes that it was worse, and I found out later the ankle had come out of the socket.

It was an emotional time. I definitely cried when I got hurt, from the pain. And getting carried off the field, there were tears then. A lot of people asked why I did the tomahawk chop when I was being carted off. Well, the doctor had said that for precautionary reasons he wanted to put my neck in a brace. And it happened on a night when my wife was back in Arkansas visiting her parents. I knew she would be watching, and who knows what she's thinking. So my first priority was to let my wife know I was OK and didn't have a spinal injury. Also, the fans had been pretty good to me, so I wanted to give them an inspirational tomahawk chop.

It was not easy sitting on the bench in the playoffs, but I was able to be a cheerleader. I'll never forget that seventh game in the playoffs. After we went up three games to one, I was talking with strength coach Frank Fultz, our weight trainer. We had decided to vote him a full share (of post-season playoff money) and here is a guy that doesn't make a whole lot. Going into that fifth game, I said to Frank, "One more victory means an extra $40,000." Then, before the sixth game, I said the same thing. But before the seventh game I didn't say anything. After Francisco Cabrera's hit, in the middle of the celebration when I'm jumping around on one leg, I yelled, "Hey Frank, an extra $40,000!"

In the Series, I remember the fifth game because of my cast. My first cast, which had been taken off and had a big tomahawk painted on it, was back in Atlanta and was going to be auctioned for charity. So I'm in my hotel room and I get a call from American SIDS Institute, and the woman says we haven't been winning because I haven't been rubbing my cast. She put the cast on the next plane to Toronto. It ended up being a pretty good gimmick. The cast got there before the game and some guys rubbed it and we won.

I really thought we would go back to Atlanta and win both games. When we were behind one run in the ninth against a guy like (Tom) Henke and (Otis) Nixon gets that big hit, I said, "Here were go again. There's no beating us now." But it didn't happen.

One guy my heart really goes out to is Charlie Leibrandt, because we would not have been there the last two years if not for him. When it was over, we just sat and watched them celebrate. We just wondered what it was like. I don't think we let anybody down not winning it. Plenty of guys have never been there, and we've been competitive in it two years in a row. We're a very good ballclub; we just haven't won the big one.

THE 1992 ATLANTA BRAVES

Greg Olson:
I looked at him [the trainer] and said, "Tell me it's just a badly sprained ankle." But I could tell by his glassy eyes that it was worse.

JONATHAN NEWTON

228

RICH MAHAN

THE 1992 ATLANTA BRAVES

No.	Date	Opponent	Result	Winner	Loser	W-L	Stg	GA/B
1.	4/7	at Houston	W 2-0	Glavine	Harnisch	1-0	1st	0.5
2.	4/8	at Houston	W 3-1	Smoltz	Kile	2-0	1st	0.5
3.	4/9	San Francisco	L 11-4	Heredia	Avery	2-1	T1st	—
4.	4/10	San Francisco	W 5-3	Leibrandt	Burba	3-1	1st	0.5
5.	4/11	San Francisco	L 3-0	Swift	Bielecki	3-2	T2nd	0.5
6.	4/12	San Francisco	W 6-2	Glavine	Downs	4-2	2nd	0.5
7.	4/12	at Cincinnati	L 5-4	Belcher	Smoltz	4-3	T2nd	1.0
8.	4/14	at Cincinnati	L 5-4	Bankhead	Freeman	4-4	3rd	2.0
9.	4/15	at Cincinnati	L 3-1	Hammond	Leibrandt	4-5	T3rd	3.0
10.	4/16	at Los Angeles	W 3-0	Bielecki	Gross	5-5	3rd	2.0
11.	4/17	at Los Angeles	L 7-5	McDowell	Peña	5-6	5th	2.0
12.	4/18	at Los Angeles	L 7-4	McDowell	Stanton	5-7	T5th	2.0
13.	4/19	at Los Angeles	L 4-2	Candiotti	Avery	5-8	6th	2.5
14.	4/20	at San Diego	W 10-4	Freeman	Lefferts	6-8	T5th	2.5
15.	4/20	at San Diego	L 4-2	Rodriguez	Bielecki	6-9	6th	2.5
16.	4/22	at San Diego	L 9-4	Hurst	Glavine	6-10	6th	3.5
17.	4/24	Houston	L 4-2	Kile	Smoltz	6-11	6th	4.5
18.	4/25	Houston	W 2-0	Avery	Portugal	7-11	6th	3.5
19.	4/26	Houston	W 3-2	Freeman	Harnisch	8-11	6th	2.5
20.	4/27	Chicago	W 5-0	Glavine	Boskie	9-11	T5th	2.0
21.	4/28	Chicago	W 1-0	Leibrandt	Castillo	10-11	5th	1.5
22.	4/29	Chicago	W 8-0	Smoltz	D.Jackson	11-11	T4th	1.0
23.	5/1	New York	L 8-7	Burke	Berenguer	11-12	5th	1.5
24.	5/2	New York	W 3-0	Glavine	Gooden	12-12	4th	1.5
25.	5/3	New York	L 7-0	Cone	Leibrandt	12-13	5th	1.5
26.	5/4	at Chicago	W 6-1	Smoltz	Castillo	13-13	T3rd	1.0
27.	5/5	at Chicago	L 4-3 (10)	McElroy	Peña	13-14	T4th	1.0
28.	5/6	at Pittsburgh	L 4-3 (16)	Patterson	Rivera	13-15	T4th	1.5
29.	5/7	at Pittsburgh	W 4-2	Glavine	Neagle	14-15	3rd	1.5
30.	5/8	at St. Louis	W 2-1	Leibrandt	Tewksbury	15-15	3rd	1.5
31.	5/9	at St. Louis	L 12-11	Perez	Freeman	15-16	4th	1.5
32.	5/10	at St. Louis	L 6-5	Agosto	Peña	15-17	4th	2.5
33.	5/11	at St. Louis	L 8-3	DeLeon	Avery	15-18	5th	3.0
34.	5/12	Pittsburgh	W 4-2	Glavine	Tomlin	16-18	4th	3.0
35.	5/13	Pittsburgh	L 11-10	Belinda	Peña	16-19	4th	4.0
36.	5/14	Pittsburgh	L 4-3	Palacios	Smoltz	16-20	4th	4.5
37.	5/15	Montreal	W 4-2	Mercker	Nabholz	17-20	4th	3.5
38.	5/16	Montreal	L 7-1	Martinez	Avery	17-21	4th	3.5
39.	5/17	Montreal	L 5-4	Hill	Glavine	17-22	T4th	4.5
40.	5/18	St. Louis	W 5-1	Leibrandt	Osborne	18-22	4th	4.0
41.	5/19	St. Louis	L 7-2	Tewksbury	Smoltz	18-23	T4th	5.0
42.	5/20	St. Louis	W 6-3	Avery	Cormier	19-23	4th	5.0
43.	5/22	at Montreal	L 7-1	Martinez	Glavine	19-24	4th	6.5
44.	5/23	at Montreal	L 7-6	Fassero	Stanton	19-25	4th	6.5
45.	5/24	at Montreal	W 2-1	Smoltz	Gardner	20-25	4th	5.5
46.	5/25	at Philadelphia	L 4-1	Mulholland	Avery	20-26	4th	6.0
47.	5/26	at Philadelphia	L 5-2	Robinson	Bielecki	20-27	6th	7.0
48.	5/27	at Philadelphia	W 9-3	Glavine	Brantley	21-27	5th	7.0
49.	5/29	at New York	W 5-1	Smoltz	Gooden	22-27	5th	5.5
50.	5/30	at New York	W 6-1	Avery	Cone	23-27	5th	5.0
51.	6/1	Philadelphia	W 7-6	Glavine	Brantley	24-27	5th	4.0
52.	6/2	Philadelphia	W 5-3	Stanton	Williams	25-27	5th	4.0
53.	6/3	Philadelphia	L 4-1	Schilling	Smoltz	25-28	5th	5.0
54.	6/5	at San Diego	W 3-2	Berenguer	Lefferts	26-28	T4th	4.5
55.	6/6	at San Diego	W 5-1	Glavine	Benes	27-28	4th	4.5
56.	6/7	at San Diego	W 9-4	Smoltz	Seminara	28-2	4th	3.5
57.	6/8	at Los Angeles	W 4-2	Leibrandt	Martinez	29-28	4th	3.5
58.	6/9	at Los Angeles	L 3-2	Hershiser	Stanton	29-29	4th	4.5
59.	6/10	at Los Angeles	W 2-1	Avery	Gross	30-29	4th	3.5
60.	6/12	San Diego	W 6-4	Berenguer	Maddux	31-29	4th	3.5
61.	6/13	San Diego	W 4-2	Smoltz	Seminara	32-29	T3rd	3.5
62.	6/14	San Diego	W 4-2	Leibrandt	Hurst	33-29	2nd	3.5
63.	6/15	Los Angeles	W 2-0	Avery	Hershiser	34-29	2nd	3.5
64.	6/16	Los Angeles	W 9-8	Berenguer	Candelaria	35-29	2nd	3.5
65.	6/17	Los Angeles	W 4-3	Glavine	Ojeda	36-29	2nd	3.5
66.	6/18	Cincinnati	L 7-5(10)	Bankhead	Stanton	36-30	2nd	4.5
67.	6/19	Cincinnati	W 3-2(10)	Mercker	Henry	37-30	2nd	3.5
68.	6/20	Cincinnati	W 2-1	Avery	Browning	38-30	2nd	2.5
69.	6/21	Cincinnati	W 2-0	Bielecki	Rijo	39-30	2nd	1.5
70.	6/23	at San Francisco	W 7-0	Glavine	Burkett	40-30	2nd	1.0
71.	6/24	at San Francisco	W 5-0	Smoltz	Wilson	41-30	2nd	1.0
72.	6/26	at Cincinnati	L 7-4	Browning	Avery	41-31	2nd	2.0
73.	6/27	at Cincinnati	L 12-3	Rijo	Leibrandt	41-32	2nd	3.0
74.	6/28	at Cincinnati	L 6-5	Charlton	Wohlers	41-33	2nd	4.0
75.	6/30	at San Francisco	W 4-3	Smoltz	Wilson	42-33	2nd	2.5
76.	7/1	at San Francisco	L 2-1	Black	Avery	42-34	2nd	2.5
77.	7/3	Chicago	W 3-0	Glavine	Boskie	43-34	2nd	2.5
78.	7/4	Chicago	W 4-2	Leibrandt	Jackson	44-34	2nd	3.0
79.	7/5	Chicago	L 8-0	Maddux	Smoltz	44-35	2nd	4.0
80.	7/6	New York	L 3-1	Cone	Freeman	44-36	2nd	5.0
81.	7/7	New York	L 5-4	Fernandez	Bielecki	44-37	2nd	6.0
82.	7/8	New York	W 2-1	Glavine	Whitehurst	45-37	2nd	5.0

No.	Date	Opponent	Result	Winner	Loser	W-L	Stg	GA/B
83.	7/9	at Chicago	W 2-0(12)	Stanton	Bullinger	46-37	2nd	5.0
84.	7/10	at Chicago	W 4-0	Smoltz	Maddux	47-37	2nd	4.0
85.	7/11	at Chicago	W 3-1	Avery	Scanlan	48-37	2nd	3.0
86.	7/12	at Chicago	W 7-4(10)	Mercker	Assenmacher	49-37	2nd	2.0
87.	7/16	at Houston	W 4-2	Avery	Williams	50-37	2nd	1.0
88.	7/17	at Houston	W 5-0	Smolz	Harnisch	51-37	2nd	1.0
89.	7/18	at Houston	W 3-0	Glavine	J.Jones	52-37	2nd	1.0
90.	7/19	at Houston	W 3-2(10)	Freeman	Hernandez	53-37	2nd	1.0
91.	7/21	at St. Louis	W 9-7	Peña	Perez	54-37	2nd	0.5
92.	7/22	at St. Louis	W 2-0	Smoltz	Olivares	55-37	1st	0.5
93.	7/24	Pittsburgh	W 4-3	Glavine	Walk	56-37	1st	2.0
94.	7/25	Pittsburgh	W 1-0	Leibrandt	D.Jackson	57-37	1st	2.0
95.	7/26	Pittsburgh	L 5-4	Belinda	Wohlers	57-38	1st	1.0
96.	7/27	Houston	L 5-1(11)	D. Jones	Pena	57-39	1st	1.0
97.	7/28	Houston	L 7-5	Harnisch	Freeman	57-40	T1st	—
98.	7/29	Houston	W 5-3	Glavine	Blair	58-40	1st	1.0
99.	7/30	at San Francisco	L 5-0	Burkett	Leibrandt	58-41	1st	0.5
100.	7/31	at San Francisco	L 4-3	Jackson	Mercker	58-42	2nd	0.5
101.	8/1	at San Francisco	W 5-3	Smoltz	Black	59-42	2nd	0.5
102	8/2	at San Francisco	W 3-0	P.Smith	Swift	60-42	T1st	—
103.		at San Francisco	W 8-5	Reynoso	Hickerson	61-42	1st	0.5
104.	8/4	Cincinnati	W 7-5	Freeman	Charlton	62-42	1st	1.5
105.	8/5	Cincinnati	W 5-1	Avery	Belcher	63-42	1st	2.5
106.	8/6	Cincinnati	W 5-3	Smoltz	Swindell	64-42	1st	3.5
107.	8/7	Los Angeles	W 6-2	Leibrandt	Gross	65-42	1st	3.5
108.	8/8	Los Angeles	W 12-2	P.Smith	Candiotti	66-42	1st	3.5
109.	8/9	Los Angeles	W 10-3	Glavine	Hershiser	67-42	1st	4.5
110.	8/10	Los Angeles	L 5-3	Martinez	Avery	67-43	1st	4.0
111.	8/11	San Diego	L 8-4	Hurst	Smoltz	67-44	1st	4.0
112.	8/13	San Diego	W 4-3	Davis	Andersen	68-44	1st	4.5
113.	8/14	at Pittsburgh	W 15-0	Glavine	Z.Smith	69-44	1st	5.5
114.	8/15	at Pittsburgh	W 7-5	Avery	D.Jackson	70-44	1st	5.5
115.	8/16	at Pittsburgh	L 4-2	Wakefield	Smoltz	70-45	1st	4.5
116.	8/17	at Pittsburgh	W 5-4	Freeman	Patterson	71-45	1st	5.0
117.	8/18	at Montreal	W 5-1	Leibrandt	Hill	72-45	1st	5.5
118.	8/19	at Montreal	W 4-2	Glavine	Nabholz	73-45	1st	6.5
119.	8/20	at Montreal	L 3-2	Fassero	Peña	73-46	1st	6.0
120.	8/21	St. Louis	L 5-2(10)	Perez	Mercker	73-47	1st	6.0
121.	8/22	St. Louis	W 3-2	P.Smith	Clark	74-47	1st	7.0
122.	8/23	St. Louis	L 8-3	Olivares	Leibrandt	74-48	1st	6.0
123.	8/25	Montreal	L 6-0	Nabholz	Glavine	74-49	1st	4.5
124.	8/26	Montreal	L 5-4	Martinez	Avery	74-50	1st	3.5
125.	8/28	at Philadelphia	L 7-3	Mulholland	Smoltz	74-51	1st	3.5
126.	8/29	at Philadelphia	W 7-6	Leibrandt	Schilling	75-51	1st	4.5
127.	8/30	at Philadelphia	L 10-2	Rivera	Glavine	75-52	1st	5.0
128.	8/31	at New York	W 8-6(14)	Wohlers	Guetterman	76-52	1st	5.5
129.		at New York	W 7-5	P.Smith	Birkbeck	77-52	1st	6.5
130.	9/1	at New York	W 4-1	Nied	Whitehurst	78-52	1st	7.5

No.	Date	Opponent	Result	Winner	Loser	W-L	Stg	GA/B
131.	9/2	at New York	L 6-5	Schourek	Smoltz	78-53	1st	7.5
132.	9/3	Montreal	L 11-2	Barnes	Leibrandt	78-54	1st	6.5
133.	9/4	Philadelphia	L 2-1	Schilling	Glavine	78-55	1st	6.5
134.	9/5	Philadelphia	W 6-5	Reardon	Williams	79-55	1st	6.5
135.	9/6	Philadelphia	W 4-3	Readron	Hartley	80-55	1st	6.5
136.	9/7	Los Angeles	W 7-1	Smoltz	Astacio	81-55	1st	6.5
137.	9/8	Los Angeles	W 7-5	Freeman	Crews	82-55	1st	7.5
138.	9/9	Cincinnati	W 12-7	Glavine	Belcher	83-55	1st	8.5
139.	9/10	Cincinnati	W 3-2	Stanton	Bankhead	84-55	1st	9.0
140.	9/11	at Houston	W 7-0	P.Smith	Kile	85-55	1st	10.0
141.	9/12	at Houston	W 9-3	Nied	Williams	86-55	1st	10.5
142.	9/13	at Houston	W 9-2	Leibrandt	Harnisch	87-55	1st	10.5
143.	9/15	at Cincinnati	L 4-2	Belcher	Avery	87-56	1st	9.5
144.	9/16	at Cincinnati	W 3-2	Stanton	Ruskin	88-56	1st	10.5
145.	9/17	at Cincinnati	L 3-2	Rijo	Smoltz	88-57	1st	9.5
146.	9/18	Houston	L 13-3	Harnisch	Leibrandt	88-58	1st	8.5
147.	9/19	Houston	L 3-2(12)	D.Jones	Freeman	88-59	1st	7.5
148.	9/20	Houston	W 16-1	Avery	Bowen	89-59	1st	7.5
149.	9/21	at Los Angeles	W 4-2	P.Smith	Hershiser	90-59	1st	8.0
150.	9/22	at Los Angeles	L 4-1	Candiotti	Smoltz	90-60	1st	6.5
151.	9/23	at San Francisco	W 7-0	Leibrandt	Black	91-60	1st	6.5
152.	9/24	at San Francisco	L 4-0	Brantley	Glavine	91-61	1st	5.5
153.	9/25	at San Diego	L 1-0	Harris	Avery	91-62	1st	4.5
154.	9/26	at San Diego	W 2-1(10)	Stanton	Rodriguez	92-62	1st	5.5
155.	9/27	at San Diego	W 2-1(10)	Reardon	Myers	93-62	1st	5.5
156.	9/29	San Francisco	W 6-0	Leibrandt	Black	94-62	1st	6.5
157.	9/30	San Francisco	L 1-0	Brantley	Glavine	94-63	1st	5.5
158.	10/1	San Francisco	W 6-5(10)	Freeman	M.Jackson	95-63	1st	6.5
159.	10/2	San Diego	W 4-1	Nied	Benes	96-63	1st	7.0
160.		San Diego	W 7-2	P.Smith	Deshaies	97-63	1st	8.0
161.	10/3	San Diego	W 1-0(6)	Leibrandt	M.Maddux	98-63	1st	8.0
162.	10/4	San Diego	L 4-3(12)	Myers	Borbon	98-64	1st	8.0

NL PLAYOFFS

	Date	Opponent	Result	Winner	Loser	W-L		
1.	10/6	Pittsburgh	W 5-1	Smoltz	Drabek	1-0		
2.	10/7	Pittsburgh	W 13-5	Avery	D.Jackson	2-0		
3.	10/9	at Pittsburgh	L 3-2	Wakefield	Glavine	2-1		
4.	10/10	at Pittsburgh	W 6-4	Smoltz	Drabek	3-1		
5.	10/11	at Pittsburgh	L 7-1	Walk	Avery	3-2		
6.	10/13	Pittsburgh	L 13-4	Wakefield	Glavine	3-3		
7.	10/14	Pittsburgh	W 3-2	Reardon	Drabek	4-3		

WORLD SERIES

	Date	Opponent	Result	Winner	Loser	W-L		
1.	10/17	Toronto	W 3-1	Glavine	Morris	1-0		
2.	10/18	Toronto	L 5-4	Ward	Reardon	1-1		
3.	10/20	at Toronto	L 3-2	Ward	Avery	1-2		
4.	10/21	at Toronto	L 2-1	Key	Glavine	1-3		
5.	10/22	at Toronto	W 7-2	Smoltz	Morris	2-3		
6.	10/24	Toronto	L 4-3(11)	Key	Leibrandt	2-4		

THE 1992 ATLANTA BRAVES

JEAN SHIFRIN